KU-756-269

THE ALEXANDER SHAKESPEARE

General Editor
R.B. Kennedy

Additional notes and editing
Mike Gould

THE TEMPEST

William Shakespeare

COLLINS

NEWHAM LIBRARIES

90800101086932

Harper Press
An imprint of HarperCollins*Publishers*
1 London Bridge Street,
London SE1 9GF

This Harper Press paperback edition published 2012

A catalogue record for this book is available from the British Library

ISBN-13: 978-0-00-790235-4

Printed and bound by CPI Group (UK) Ltd, Croydon, CR0 4YY

MIX
Paper from
responsible sources
FSC® C007454

FSC™ is a non-profit international organisation established to promote
the responsible management of the world's forests. Products carrying the
FSC label are independently certified to assure consumers that they come
from forests that are managed to meet the social, economic and
ecological needs of present and future generations,
and other controlled sources.

Find out more about HarperCollins and the environment at
www.harpercollins.co.uk/green

Life & Times section © HarperCollins*Publishers* Ltd
Gerard Cheshire asserts his moral rights as author of the Life & Times section
Shakespeare: Words and Phrases adapted from
Collins English Dictionary
Typesetting in Kalix by Palimpsest Book Production Limited,
Falkirk, Stirlingshire

All rights reserved. No part of this publication may be reproduced,
stored in a retrieval system, or transmitted, in any form or by any means,
electronic, mechanical, photocopying, recording or otherwise,
without the prior permission of the publishers.

This book is sold subject to the condition that it shall not, by way of trade
or otherwise, be lent, re-sold, hired out or otherwise circulated without the
publisher's prior consent in any form of binding or cover other than that
in which it is published and without a similar condition including
this condition being imposed on the subsequent purchaser.

9

Prefatory Note

This Shakespeare play uses the full Alexander text. By keeping in mind the fact that the language has changed considerably in four hundred years, as have customs, jokes, and stage conventions, the editors have aimed at helping the modern reader – whether English is their mother tongue or not – to grasp the full significance of the play. The Notes, intended primarily for examination candidates, are presented in a simple, direct style. The needs of those unfamiliar with British culture have been specially considered.

Since quiet study of the printed word is unlikely to bring fully to life plays that were written directly for the public theatre, attention has been drawn to dramatic effects which are important in performance. The editors see Shakespeare's plays as living works of art which can be enjoyed today on stage, film and television in many parts of the world.

CONTENTS

An Elizabethan playhouse. Note the apron stage protruding into the auditorium, the space below it, the inner room at the rear of the stage, the gallery above the inner stage, the canopy over the main stage, and the absence of a roof over the audience.

The Theatre in Shakespeare's Day

On the face of it, the conditions in the Elizabethan theatre were not such as to encourage great writers. The public playhouse itself was not very different from an ordinary inn-yard; it was open to the weather; among the spectators were often louts, pickpockets and prostitutes; some of the actors played up to the rowdy elements in the audience by inserting their own jokes into the authors' lines, while others spoke their words loudly but unfeelingly; the presentation was often rough and noisy, with fireworks to represent storms and battles, and a table and a few chairs to represent a tavern; there were no actresses, so boys took the parts of women, even such subtle and mature ones as Cleopatra and Lady Macbeth; there was rarely any scenery at all in the modern sense. In fact, a quick inspection of the English theatre in the reign of Elizabeth I by a time-traveller from the twentieth century might well produce only one positive reaction: the costumes were often elaborate and beautiful.

Shakespeare himself makes frequent comments in his plays about the limitations of the playhouse and the actors of his time, often apologizing for them. At the beginning of *Henry V* the Prologue refers to the stage as 'this unworthy scaffold' and to the theatre building (the Globe, probably) as 'this wooden O', and emphasizes the urgent need for imagination in making up for all the deficiencies of presentation. In introducing Act IV the Chorus goes so far as to say:

> . . . we shall much disgrace
> With four or five most vile and ragged foils,
> Right ill-dispos'd in brawl ridiculous,
> The name of Agincourt, (lines 49–52)

In *A Midsummer Night's Dream* (Act V, Scene i) he seems to dismiss actors with the words:

The best in this kind are but shadows.

Yet Elizabeth's theatre, with all its faults, stimulated dramatists to a variety of achievement that has never been equalled and, in Shakespeare, produced one of the greatest writers in history. In spite of all his grumbles he seems to have been fascinated by the challenge that it presented him with. It is necessary to re-examine his theatre carefully in order to understand how he was able to achieve so much with the materials he chose to use. What sort of place was the Elizabethan playhouse in reality? What sort of people were these criticized actors? And what sort of audiences gave them their living?

The Development of the Theatre up to Shakespeare's Time

For centuries in England noblemen had employed groups of skilled people to entertain them when required. Under Tudor rule, as England became more secure and united, actors such as these were given more freedom, and they often performed in public, while still acknowledging their 'overlords' (in the 1570s, for example, when Shakespeare was still a schoolboy at Stratford, one famous company was called 'Lord Leicester's Men'). London was rapidly becoming larger and more important in the second half of the sixteenth century, and many of the companies of actors took the opportunities offered to establish themselves at inns on the main roads leading to the City (for example, the Boar's Head in Whitechapel and the Tabard in South-wark) or in the City itself. These groups of actors would come to an agreement with the inn-keeper which would give them the use of the yard for their performances after people had eaten and drunk well in the middle of the day. Before long, some inns were taken over completely by companies of players and thus became the first public theatres. In 1574 the officials of the City of London issued an order which shows clearly that these theatres were both popular and also offensive to some respectable people, because the order complains about 'the inordinate haunting of great multitudes of people, specially youth, to plays interludes and shows; namely occasion of frays and quarrels, evil practices of incontinency in great inns . . .' There is evidence that, on public holidays, the theatres on the banks of the Thames were crowded with noisy apprentices and tradesmen, but it would be wrong to think that audiences were always undiscriminating and loudmouthed. In spite of the disapproval of Puritans and the more staid members of society, by the 1590s, when Shakespeare's plays were beginning to be performed, audiences consisted of a good cross-section of English society, nobility as well as workers, intellectuals as well as simple people out for a laugh; also (and in this respect English theatres were unique in Europe), it was quite normal for respectable women to attend plays. So Shakespeare had to write plays which would appeal to people of widely different kinds. He had to provide 'something for everyone' but at the same time to take care to unify the material so that it would not seem to fall into separate pieces as they watched it. A speech like that of the drunken porter in *Macbeth* could provide the 'groundlings' with a belly-laugh, but also held a deeper significance for those who could appreciate it. The audience he wrote for was one of a number of apparent drawbacks which Shakespeare was able to turn to his and our advantage.

Shakespeare's Actors

Nor were all the actors of the time mere 'rogues, vagabonds and sturdy beggars' as some were described in a Statute of 1572. It is true that many of them had a hard life and earned very little money, but leading actors could become partners in the ownership of the theatres in which they acted: Shakespeare was a shareholder in the Globe and the Blackfriars theatres when he was an actor as well as a playwright. In any case, the attacks made on Elizabethan actors were usually directed at their morals and not at their acting ability; it is clear that many of them must have been good at their trade if they were able to interpret complex works like the great tragedies in such a way as to attract enthusiastic audiences. Undoubtedly some of the boys took the women's parts with skill and confidence, since a man called Coryate, visiting Venice in 1611, expressed surprise that women could act as well as they: 'I saw women act, a thing that I never saw before . . . and they performed it with as good a grace, action, gesture . . . as ever I saw any masculine actor.' The quality of most of the actors who first presented Shakespeare's plays is probably accurately summed up by Fynes Moryson, who wrote, '. . . as there be, in my opinion, more plays in London than in all the parts of the world I have seen, so do these players or comedians excel all other in the world.'

The Structure of the Public Theatre

Although the 'purpose-built' theatres were based on the inn-yards which had been used for play-acting, most of them were circular. The walls contained galleries on three storeys from which the wealthier patrons watched, they must have been something like the 'boxes' in a modern theatre, except that they held much larger numbers – as many as 1500. The 'groundlings' stood on the floor of the building, facing a raised stage which projected from the 'stage-wall', the main features of which were:

1 a small room opening on to the back of the main stage and on the same level as it (rear stage),
2 a gallery above this inner stage (upper stage),
3 canopy projecting from above the gallery over the main stage, to protect the actors from the weather (the 700 or 800 members of the audience who occupied the yard, or 'pit' as we call it today, had the sky above them).

In addition to these features there were dressing-rooms behind the stage and a space underneath it from which entrances could be made through trap-doors. All the acting areas – main stage, rear stage, upper stage and under stage – could be entered by actors directly from their dressing rooms, and all of them were used in productions of Shakespeare's plays. For example, the inner stage, an almost cavelike structure, would have been where Ferdinand and Miranda are 'discovered' playing chess in the last act of *The Tempest*, while the upper stage was certainly the balcony from which Romeo climbs down in Act III of *Romeo and Juliet*.

It can be seen that such a building, simple but adaptable, was not really unsuited to the presentation of plays like Shakespeare's. On the contrary, its simplicity guaranteed the minimum of distraction, while its shape and construction must have produced a sense of involvement on the part of the audience that modern producers would envy.

Other Resources of the Elizabethan Theatre

Although there were few attempts at scenery in the public theatre (painted backcloths were occasionally used in court performances), Shakespeare and his fellow playwrights were able to make use of a fair variety of 'properties', lists of such articles have survived: they include beds, tables, thrones, and also trees, walls, a gallows, a Trojan horse and a 'Mouth of Hell'; in a list of properties belonging to the manager, Philip Henslowe, the curious item 'two mossy banks' appears. Possibly one of them was used for the

> bank whereon the wild thyme blows,
> Where oxlips and the nodding violet grows

in *A Midsummer Night's Dream* (Act II, Scene i). Once again, imagination must have been required of the audience.

Costumes were the one aspect of stage production in which

trouble and expense were hardly ever spared to obtain a magnificent effect. Only occasionally did they attempt any historical accuracy (almost all Elizabethan productions were what we should call 'modern-dress' ones), but they were appropriate to the characters who wore them: kings were seen to be kings and beggars were similarly unmistakable. It is an odd fact that there was usually no attempt at illusion in the costuming: if a costume looked fine and rich it probably was. Indeed, some of the costumes were almost unbelievably expensive. Henslowe lent his company £19 to buy a cloak, and the Alleyn brothers, well-known actors, gave £20 for a 'black velvet cloak, with sleeves embroidered all with silver and gold, lined with black satin striped with gold'.

With the one exception of the costumes, the 'machinery' of the playhouse was economical and uncomplicated rather than crude and rough, as we can see from this second and more leisurely look at it. This meant that playwrights were stimulated to produce the imaginative effects that they wanted from the language that they used. In the case of a really great writer like Shakespeare, when he had learned his trade in the theatre as an actor, it seems that he received quite enough assistance of a mechanical and structural kind without having irksome restrictions and conventions imposed on him; it is interesting to try to guess what he would have done with the highly complex apparatus of a modern television studio. We can see when we look back to his time that he used his instrument, the Elizabethan theatre, to the full, but placed his ultimate reliance on the communication between his imagination and that of his audience through the medium of words. It is, above all, his rich and wonderful use of language that must have made play-going at that time a memorable experience for people of widely different kinds. Fortunately, the deep satisfaction of appreciating and enjoying Shakespeare's work can be ours also, if we are willing to overcome the language difficulty produced by the passing of time.

Shakespeare: A Timeline

Very little indeed is known about Shakespeare's private life; the facts included here are almost the only indisputable ones. The dates of Shakespeare's plays are those on which they were first produced.

1558   Queen Elizabeth crowned.

1561   Francis Bacon born.

1564   Christopher Marlowe born.   William Shakespeare born, April 23rd, baptized April 26th.

1566   Shakespeare's brother, Gilbert, born.

1567   Mary, Queen of Scots, deposed.
       James VI (later James I of England) crowned King of Scotland.

1572   Ben Jonson born.
       Lord Leicester's Company (of players) licensed; later called Lord Strange's, then the Lord Chamberlain's and finally (under James) the King's Men.

1573   John Donne born.

1574   The Common Council of London directs that all plays and playhouses in London must be licensed.

1576   James Burbage builds the first public playhouse, The Theatre, at Shoreditch, outside the walls of the City.

1577   Francis Drake begins his voyage round the world (completed 1580).
       Holinshed's Chronicles of England, Scotland and Ireland published (which

Shakespeare later used extensively).

1582		Shakespeare married to Anne Hathaway.
1583	The Queen's Company founded by royal warrant.	Shakespeare's daughter, Susanna, born.
1585		Shakespeare's twins, Hamnet and Judith, born.
1586	Sir Philip Sidney, the Elizabethan ideal 'Christian knight', poet, patron, soldier, killed at Zutphen in the Low Countries.	
1587	Mary, Queen of Scots, beheaded. Marlowe's *Tamburlaine (Part I)* first staged.	
1588	Defeat of the Spanish Armada. Marlowe's *Tamburlaine (Part II)* first staged.	
1589	Marlowe's *Jew of Malta* and Kyd's *Spanish Tragedy* (a 'revenge tragedy' and one of the most popular plays of Elizabethan times).	
1590	Spenser's *Faerie Queene* (Books I–III) published.	
1592	Marlowe's *Doctor Faustus* and *Edward II* first staged. Witchcraft trials in Scotland. Robert Greene, a rival playwright, refers to Shakespeare as 'an upstart crow' and 'the only Shake-scene in a country'.	*Titus Andronicus* *Henry VI, Parts I, II and III* *Richard III*
1593	London theatres closed by the plague. Christopher Marlowe killed in a Deptford tavern.	*Two Gentlemen of Verona* *Comedy of Errors* *The Taming of the Shrew* *Love's Labour's Lost*
1594	Shakespeare's company becomes The Lord Chamberlain's Men.	*Romeo and Juliet*

1595	Raleigh's first expedition to Guiana. Last expedition of Drake and Hawkins (both died).	*Richard II* *A Midsummer Night's Dream*
1596	Spenser's *Faerie Queene* (Books IV–VI) published. James Burbage buys rooms at Blackfriars and begins to convert them into a theatre.	*King John* *The Merchant of Venice* Shakespeare's son Hamnet dies. Shakespeare's father is granted a coat of arms.
1597	James Burbage dies, his son Richard, a famous actor, turns the Blackfriars Theatre into a private playhouse.	*Henry IV (Part I)* Shakespeare buys and redecorates New Place at Stratford.
1598	Death of Philip II of Spain	*Henry IV (Part II)* *Much Ado About Nothing*
1599	Death of Edmund Spenser. The Globe Theatre completed at Bankside by Richard and Cuthbert Burbage.	*Henry V* *Julius Caesar* *As You Like It*
1600	Fortune Theatre built at Cripplegate. East India Company founded for the extension of English trade and influence in the East. The Children of the Chapel begin to use the hall at Blackfriars.	*Merry Wives of Windsor* *Troilus and Cressida*
1601		*Hamlet*
1602	Sir Thomas Bodley's library opened at Oxford.	*Twelfth Night*
1603	Death of Queen Elizabeth. James I comes to the throne. Shakespeare's company becomes The King's Men. Raleigh tried, condemned and sent to the Tower	
1604	Treaty of peace with Spain	*Measure for Measure* *Othello* *All's Well that Ends Well*
1605	The Gunpowder Plot: an attempt by a group of Catholics to blow up the Houses of Parliament.	

1606	Guy Fawkes and other plotters executed.	*Macbeth* *King Lear*
1607	Virginia, in America, colonized. A great frost in England.	*Antony and Cleopatra* *Timon of Athens* *Coriolanus* Shakespeare's daughter, Susanna, married to Dr. John Hall.
1608	The company of the Children of the Chapel Royal (who had performed at Blackfriars for ten years) is disbanded. John Milton born. Notorious pirates executed in London.	Richard Burbage leases the Blackfriars Theatre to six of his fellow actors, including Shakespeare. *Pericles, Prince of Tyre*
1609		Shakespeare's Sonnets published.
1610	A great drought in England	*Cymbeline*
1611	Chapman completes his great translation of the *Iliad*, the story of Troy. Authorized Version of the Bible published.	*A Winter's Tale* *The Tempest*
1612	Webster's *The White Devil* first staged.	Shakespeare's brother, Gilbert, dies.
1613	Globe theatre burnt down during a performance of *Henry VIII* (the firing of small cannon set fire to the thatched roof). Webster's *Duchess of Malfi* first staged.	*Henry VIII* *Two Noble Kinsmen* Shakespeare buys a house at Blackfriars.
1614	Globe Theatre rebuilt in 'far finer manner than before'.	
1616	Ben Jonson publishes his plays in one volume. Raleigh released from the Tower in order to prepare an expedition to the gold mines of Guiana.	Shakespeare's daughter, Judith, marries Thomas Quiney. Death of Shakespeare on his birthday, April 23rd.
1618	Raleigh returns to England and is executed on the charge for which he was imprisoned in 1603.	
1623	Publication of the Folio edition of Shakespeare's plays	Death of Anne Shakespeare (née Hathaway).

Life & Times

William Shakespeare the Playwright

There exists a curious paradox when it comes to the life of William Shakespeare. He easily has more words written about him than any other famous English writer, yet we know the least about him. This inevitably means that most of what is written about him is either fabrication or speculation. The reason why so little is known about Shakespeare is that he wasn't a novelist or a historian or a man of letters. He was a playwright, and playwrights were considered fairly low on the social pecking order in Elizabethan society. Writing plays was about providing entertainment for the masses – the great unwashed. It was the equivalent to being a journalist for a tabloid newspaper.

In fact, we only know of Shakespeare's work because two of his friends had the foresight to collect his plays together following his death and have them printed. The only reason they did so was apparently because they rated his talent and thought it would be a shame if his words were lost.

Consequently his body of work has ever since been assessed and reassessed as the greatest contribution to English literature. That is despite the fact that we know that different printers took it upon themselves to heavily edit the material they worked from. We also know that Elizabethan plays were worked and reworked frequently, so that they evolved over time until they were honed to perfection, which means that many different hands played their part in the active writing process. It would therefore be fair to say that any play attributed to Shakespeare is unlikely to contain a great deal of original input. Even the plots were based on well known historical events, so it would be hard to know what fragments of any Shakespeare play came from that single mind.

One might draw a comparison with the Christian bible, which remains such a compelling read because it came from the collaboration of many contributors and translators over centuries, who each adjusted the stories until they could no longer be improved. As virtually nothing is known of Shakespeare's life and even less about his method of working, we shall never know the truth about his plays. They certainly contain some very elegant phrasing, clever plot devices and plenty of words never before seen in print, but as to whether Shakespeare invented them from a unique imagination or whether he simply took them from others around him is anyone's guess.

The best bet seems to be that Shakespeare probably took the lead role in devising the original drafts of the plays, but was open to collaboration from any source when it came to developing them into workable scripts for effective performances. He would have had to work closely with his fellow actors in rehearsals, thereby finding out where to edit, abridge, alter, reword and so on.

In turn, similar adjustments would have occurred in his absence, so that definitive versions of his plays never really existed. In effect Shakespeare was only responsible for providing the framework of plays, upon which others took liberties over time. This wasn't helped by the fact that the English language itself was not definitive at that time either. The consequence was that people took it upon themselves to spell words however they pleased or to completely change words and phrasing to suit their own preferences.

It is easy to see then, that Shakespeare's plays were always going to have lives of their own, mutating and distorting in detail like Chinese whispers. The culture of creative preservation was simply not established in Elizabethan England. Creative ownership of Shakespeare's plays was lost to him as soon as he released them into the consciousness of others. They saw nothing wrong with taking his ideas and running with them, because no one had ever suggested that one shouldn't, and Shakespeare probably regarded his work in the same way. His plays weren't sacrosanct works of art, they were templates for theatre folk to make their livings from, so they had every right to mould them into productions that drew in the crowds as effectively as possible. Shakespeare was like the helmsman of a sailing ship, steering the vessel but wholly reliant on the team work of his crew to arrive at the desired destination.

It seems that Shakespeare certainly had a natural gift, but the genius of his plays may be attributable to the collective efforts of Shakespeare and others. It is a rather satisfying notion to think that *his* plays might actually be the creative outpourings of the Elizabethan milieu in which Shakespeare immersed himself. That makes them important social documents as well as seminal works of the English language.

Money in Shakespeare's Day

It is extremely difficult, if not impossible, to relate the value of money in our time to its value in another age and to compare prices of commodities today and in the past. Many items *are* simply not comparable on grounds of quality or serviceability.

There was a bewildering variety of coins in use in Elizabethan England. As nearly all English and European coins were gold or silver, they had intrinsic value apart from their official value. This meant that foreign coins circulated freely in England and were officially recognized, for example the French crown (écu) worth about 30p (72 cents), and the Spanish ducat worth about 33p (79 cents). The following table shows some of the coins mentioned by Shakespeare and their relation to one another.

GOLD	British	American	SILVER	British	American
sovereign (heavy type)	£1.50	$3.60	shilling	10p	24c
sovereign (light type)	66p–£1	$1.58–$2.40	groat	1.5p	4c
angel					
royal	33p–50p	79c–$1.20			
noble	50p	$1.20			
crown	25p	60c			

A comparison of the following prices in Shakespeare's time with the prices of the same items today will give some idea of the change in the value of money.

ITEM	PRICE British	American	ITEM	PRICE British	American
beef, per lb.	0.5p	1c	cherries (lb.)	1p	2c
mutton, leg	7.5p	18c	7 oranges	1p	2c
rabbit	3.5p	9c	1 lemon	1p	2c
chicken	3p	8c	cream (quart)	2.5p	6c
potatoes (lb)	10p	24c	sugar (lb.)	£1	$2.40
carrots (bunch)	1p	2c	sack (wine) (gallon)	14p	34c
8 artichokes	4p	9c	tobacco (oz.)	25p	60c
1 cucumber	1p	2c	biscuits (lb.)	12.5p	30c

INTRODUCTION

The Tempest, like any work of art, was partly conditioned by the times and circumstances in which it was created. It was written at the end of Shakespeare's career in the theatre and contains many of the themes which appear in his earlier plays. Nevertheless it shows new features and fresh experimentation with dramatic forms. Writers have suggested that in the epilogue he is bidding farewell to the stage before retiring to Stratford, and this may be so. It is certainly tempting to see in the magician Prospero the artist Shakespeare. But whether or not we think that there are autobiographical references in the play, it may be useful to try to look over Shakespeare's shoulder as he begins this play and so increase our understanding of what *The Tempest* is about.

We can start with its title. In 1609 nine ships were on their way from England carrying five hundred colonists to Virginia when a hurricane hit the little fleet; the flag-ship *Sea Adventure* was wrecked off the Bermudas but the passengers and crew miraculously managed to get ashore safely. They rebuilt the ship and reached their destination the following year. The contemporary account by Strachey (see Appendix) almost certainly set Shakespeare's mind working. In the early 17th century the New World of the American continent was exciting men's imaginations as vividly as space exploration excites our imaginations today – and perhaps even more hopefully. Here perhaps lay a chance for men to make a fresh start, to leave behind a bad old past. The ideas of discovery and of self-discovery are central to the play.

If Strachey's account stimulated Shakespeare's first ideas for the play, a contemporary theatrical fashion influenced him in many of its features. This was the Masque, an indoor fantasy-entertainment which had developed at the Court and in private theatres and which contrasted quite sharply with the more realistic drama of the public theatres. Plot characterization and dialogue were less important than spectacular scenery, splendid costumes, musical effects, songs, dancing, and stately verse. A rough comparison might be made between straight drama and opera or ballet in the theatre today. The masque was an aristocratic and artificial form of drama in which the ideal was more important than the real, ideas than characters. It often celebrated a special occasion, such as a royal wedding. Not only does *The Tempest* contain a mini-masque (to celebrate the betrothal of the royal lovers in the play) but it is often masque-like in itself, with its spectacular storm-scene, supernatural music, magician's banquet, and exotic characters such as the spirit Ariel and the grotesque savage Caliban. Masques make a strong appeal to eyes and ears, and this is more obviously true of *The Tempest* than of any other Shakespeare play.

The masque-influence in the play extends to the characters and to the setting. It would certainly not be true to say that the characters are lacking in reality and are simply two-dimensional 'types' or flat caricatures; much of the verse dialogue is as natural as everyday speech and there is a dramatic narrative within which they can develop. But the play is a very short one (about half the length of *Hamlet*, for instance) and its compression does cramp characterization. Perhaps this was Shakespeare's deliberate intention at the outset: this was to be a play in which themes were to be more important than characters, and *kinds* of people were to be shown rather than individuals.

The setting contributes to the 'distancing' effect of the masque, as if we were on a different plane of existence while watching the play. At the beginning and end of *The Tempest* it is true that we are in the real world of ships and simple mariners, but on the island itself we are in the realm of fantasy, though that dream-world has the vividness and clarity of a dream which seems more real than the existence to which we return when we wake up – or leave the theatre. This feeling of being in a dream is contributed to by the number of references to sleep and waking there are in the play.

The Tempest is not only a very short play but it is one of Shakespeare's most neatly organized. Whereas the action in his other plays spreads and sprawls like life itself over a period of time, this is constructed, like classical drama, within the tight framework of the 'unities' of time, place and action (the plot and characters). The events on the island take place in the afternoon between two and six o'clock, 'stage-time' and 'audience-time' being almost identical. Once on the island the characters remain there throughout the play and are therefore in a sense in one place. And although there are three 'plots' developing simultaneously, they are moving to a common conclusion, and with a strong feeling of unity, under Prospero's control.

An interesting effect of this compression is to emphasize the importance of time in the play: the events which precede the play and are only referred to – the usurpation of Prospero by his brother Antonio in far-off Milan twelve long years ago; the wedding of Claribel in distant Tunis from which Alonso's court are returning to Naples – these are made to seem remote in time and space. Just as the island, like any island, appears even more detached from the world than it actually is, so has time seemed on the island. But suddenly destiny has brought together those who thought that the past was dead; those great distances of time and space had shrunk to the size of a small island and the urgency of a few hours.

What is *The Tempest* 'about'? The summing-up will suggest some thoughts about the characters and the themes which they develop, in answering this question; and in an Introduction only a few broad hints are required. It has already been suggested that the play is about discovery and self-discovery: those who come to Prospero's island, like the lovers who come to the wood near Athens in that other dream-play, *A Midsummer Night's Dream*, make discoveries about each other and about themselves which change their lives. Even the 'presiding deity' of the island, Prospero himself, makes discoveries. Magician he may be, but he is also a developing human being. It is a play about metamorphosis or change, about how our lives can be dramatically transformed, for example when we suddenly and it seems miraculously fall in love, or when a truth is suddenly revealed to our understanding. It is a play about being imprisoned, not only physically but within the limitations of our understanding, or of our own natures, and about being released from that bondage. It is about the need for self-control and the discipline of education if we are to become masters of any art or science, masters of other people, or (above all) masters of ourselves. These themes insistently weave their way to and fro through the language and imagery of a play in which the sense of revelation is perhaps the key emotion. If the play expresses a single feeling, it is 'How strange life is! And how wonderful.'

LIST OF CHARACTERS

Alonso	King of Naples
Sebastian	his brother
Prospero	the right Duke of Milan
Antonio	his brother, the usurping Duke of Milan
Ferdinand	son to the King of Naples
Gonzalo	an honest old counsellor
Adrian *Francisco*	Lords
Caliban	a savage and deformed slave
Trinculo	a jester
Stephano	a drunken butler
Master of a ship	
Boatswain	
Mariners	
Miranda	daughter to Prospero
Ariel	an airy spirit
Iris *Ceres* *Juno* *Nymphs* *Reapers*	spirits
Other Spirits	attending on Prospero

The Scene: A ship at sea; afterwards an uninhabited island

ACT I, SCENE I

The first scene of the play, the only one not to take place on the island itself, opens with a vivid and realistic storm. The sound of thunder and the flashes of lightning plunge the audience into the play without warning or introduction. It is a scene of mounting panic and confusion in which, although we are given brief impressions of the characters of the king and his court by their reactions to danger, we are not told their names.

The Shipmaster is the Captain of the vessel, and the Boatswain is his chief assistant. In Shakespeare's theatre, they would have probably entered respectively on the upper and lower stage levels, the Master shouting from the poop deck to the Boatswain on the main deck.

2. *what cheer?* How's it going?

3. *yarely* briskly.
4. *bestir* look lively! Move!
4–5. *bestir . . . yare* the urgency of these repeated words is further emphasized by the short, sharp, imperative sentences in the scene (i.e see 'Take in the topsail'). The Boatswain follows the Master's lead and mixes encouraging phrases with crisp commands.

6. *Take in the topsail* i.e. to prevent the ship being blown further in towards the shore.
6. *Tend to* pay attention to.
6. *master's whistle* used only by the Master, to control his crew's management of the ship.
7–8. *Blow . . . enough* perhaps the whistle has just blown, and the Boatswain then shouts at the storm to burst its lungs with blowing, provided that the ship has enough sea-room in which to move.
Stage Direction. *Enter Alonso etc.* The fine court robes worn by the King and his courtiers, make it clear they are quite different from the crew, as do their clumsy, ineffective movements which contrast with the mariners' businesslike actions.
10. *Play the men* Alonso either means, 'Behave like men', or he is urging the busy Boatswain to 'Play the men' i.e. work them hard – a rather unnecessary piece of advice in the circumstances!

ACT ONE
Scene I

*On a ship at sea; a tempestuous noise of thunder
and lightning heard.*

[Enter a SHIPMASTER *and a* BOATSWAIN*]*

Shipmaster
Boatswain!
Boatswain
Here, master; what cheer?
Shipmaster
Good! Speak to th' mariners; fall to 't yarely, or we
run ourselves aground; bestir, bestir.

[Exit]

[Enter MARINERS*]*

Boatswain
Heigh, my hearts! cheerly, cheerly, my hearts! yare,   5
yare! Take in the topsail. Tend to th' master's
whistle. Blow till thou burst thy wind, if room
enough.

[Enter ALONSO, SEBASTIAN, ANTONIO, FERDINAND,
GONZALO *and others]*

Alonso
Good boatswain, have care. Where's the master?
Play the men.   10
Boatswain
I pray now, keep below.
Antonio
Where is the master, Botswain?

13. *Do . . . him?* can't you hear his whistle?
13. *You mar our labour* you are spoiling our efforts.

15. *Nay, good, be patient* Gonzalo's role in life is to be diplomatic, as Alonso's chief counsellor.
16. *roarers* the sound of the waves raging.

18. *whom thou hast aboard* i.e. the king, therefore take extra care.

19–20. *You are a counsellor* Gonzalo is a 'counsellor' in that he gives advice, but he is also a 'councillor', a member of Alonso's Privy Council.
21. *present* present moment.
22. *hand* handle.
24. *make* yourself *ready* prepare yourself by prayer (for death, if need be).
25. *mischance of the hour* misfortune that may occur at any moment.
27. *comfort* reassurance.
28. *drowning-mark* birth-mark or mole. (Such moles or marks were superstitiously believed to predict how a man would die.)
28. *complexion* facial appearance, or, perhaps temperament.
29. *perfect gallows* i.e. is a sure sign that he will be hanged rather than die in any other way. (This refers to the proverb that 'he that is born to be hanged will never be drowned'.)
9–31. *Stand . . . advantage* Stick to your word, dear Mistress Fortune, that the Boatswain is going to be hanged, and make sure that the rope from which he will swing become our lifeline, as our own is not much use in this storm.
30. *cable* anchor rope.
32. *our case is miserable* our position is hopeless.
33. *Down with the topmast* the topsail has already been taken down after being furled, and the next step is to lower the topmast.
33–4. *Bring . . . maincourse* the dangerous, drifting movement towards the shore has been partly halted by lowering the topsail and topmast, now the Boatswain attempts to heave-to (try) by using the mainsail (*maincourse*) to control the ship.
35–6. *louder . . . office* the passengers' cries are louder than the storm or our shouts as we do our work.

Boatswain

Do you not hear him? You mar our labour, keep your
cabins; you do assist the storm.

Gonzalo

Nay, good, be patient.   15

Boatswain

When the sea is. Hence! What cares these roarers for
the name of king? To cabin! silence! Trouble us not.

Gonzalo

Good, yet remember whom thou hast aboard.

Boatswain

None that I more love than myself. You are a
counsellor; if you can command these elements to   20
silence, and work the peace of the present, we will
not hand a rope more. Use your authority; if you
cannot, give thanks you have liv'd so long, and make
yourself ready in your cabin for the mischance of the
hour, if it so hap. – Cheerly, good hearts! – Out of   25
our way, I say.

[Exit]

Gonzalo

I have great comfort from this fellow. Methinks he
hath no drowning mark upon him; his complexion is
perfect gallows. Stand fast, good Fate, to his hanging;
make the rope of his destiny our cable, for our own   30
doth little advantage. If he be not born to be hang'd,
our case is miserable.

[Exeunt]

[Re-enter BOATSWAIN]

Boatswain

Down with the topmast. Yare, lower, lower! Bring her
to try wi' th' maincourse. *[A cry within]* A plague upon
this howling! They are louder than the weather or our   35
office.

37. *give o'er* stop working.

42. *whoreson* filthy (lit. 'You bastard', i.e. son of a prostitute).

45. *I'll . . . drowning* I guarantee he won't drown.

46–7. *as . . . wench* possibly 'As easy as a whore' which sounds a rather crude simile to come from Gonzalo's lips.

48. *Lay her a-hold* i.e. bring her bows into the wind to prevent any further movement towards the shore.

48. *set her two courses* set the ship's foresail and mainsail. (This last, desperate measure is to get the ship moving again at such an angle that the vessel tacks away from the shore instead of being blown on to it.)

48–9. *off to sea again* i.e. instead of getting any further inshore.

51. *What . . . cold?* 'A cold mouth' is an image of death, but the Boatswain may be taking a final swig from his flask to keep himself warm when he is plunged into the cold sea, or taking a last leave of the crew, drinking to each other.

52. *Prince* i.e. Ferdinand.

52. *assist* wait upon. (Even in the dangerous situation, Gonzalo remains the loyal counsellor, whose place is at the King's side.)

52–63. Verse follows the prose used by the working men, to distinguish the courtiers, though it is ironical that the apparently more dignified Sebastian and Antonio (in their speech and costume) should be more abusive and behave less well than their inferiors.

54. *merely* completely.

55. *wide-chopp'd* wide-mouthed (partly because he has been drinking, and partly because he has been both shouting orders and answering the nobles back).

56. *ten tides* pirates were hanged at low-water mark and left there until three tides had washed over them.

[Re-enter SEBASTIAN, ANTONIO, *and* GONZALO*]*

Yet again! What do you here? Shall we give o'er,
and drown? Have you a mind to sink?

Sebastian

A pox o' your throat, you bawling, blasphemous,
incharitable dog!   40

Boatswain

Work you, then.

Antonio

Hang, cur, hang, you whoreson, insolent noise-maker;
we are less afraid to be drown'd than thou art.

Gonzalo

I'll warrant him for drowning, though the ship were no
stronger than a nutshell, and as leaky as an unstanched   45
wench.

Boatswain

Lay her a-hold, a-hold; set her two courses; off to sea
again; lay her off.

[Enter MARINERS, *wet]*

Mariners

All lost! to prayers, to prayers! all lost!

[Exeunt]

Boatswain

What, must our mouths be cold?   50

Gonzalo

The King and Prince at prayers! Let's assist them,
For our case is as theirs.

Sebastian

                                I am out of patience.

Antonio

We are merely cheated of our lives by drunkards.
This wide-chopp'd rascal – would thou mightst lie
drowning   55
The washing of ten tides!

57–8. Though . . . him the sound of these lines creates the suck and gurgle of the sea's waves.

57. swear against i.e. every soldier *(drop)* in Neptune's army takes an oath not to allow him to escape to be hanged rather than drowned.

58. at wid'st as widely as possible.

58. glut swallow.

60–1. We split the ship's breaking up!

62–3. King . . . him although Alonso has spoken only once, and been seen only briefly, we are continually reminded of his presence.

64–7. Now . . . death Gonzalo would willingly exchange any amount of sea for one acre of unproductive heathland. This reference to dry land not only prepares us for the next scene but also increases our feeling that the stage is a ship at sea.

65. furze gorse.

66–7. The wills . . . death Gonzalo, while submitting with Christian patience to the wishes of the heavenly powers, would nevertheless prefer not to die by drowning.

This opening scene expresses the play's title in visual form and allows us revealing glimpses of some of the characters. It also establishes the idea of chaos and disorder in the human world, which Prospero will use when it suits him throughout the remainder of the play.

Gonzalo

                      He'll be hang'd yet,
Though every drop of water swear against it,
And gape at wid'st to glut him.
[A confused noise within: 'Mercy on us!' –
'We split, we split!' – 'Farewell, my wife and children!' –   60
'Farewell, brother!' – 'We split, we split, we split!']

Antonio

Let's all sink wi' th' King. Sebastian
Let's take leave of him.

        [Exeunt ANTONIO *and* SEBASTIAN*]*

Gonzalo

Now would I give a thousand furlongs of sea for an
acre of barren ground – long heath, brown furze,   65
any thing. The wills above be done, but I would fain
die a dry death.

        [Exeunt]

SCENE II

The second scene, a long one, contrasts sharply with what we have just witnessed. It answers questions, presents its characters in 'close-up' detail, and introduces the setting of the play and its central situation.

It is divided into four phases. In phase one (lines 1–186), Prospero tells Miranda about the shipwreck and reveals its link to past events. In phase two (lines 187–304), Prospero reminds Ariel of his past and promises him freedom in the near future; in phase three (lines 305–74), Caliban angrily protests against Prospero's past and present treatment of him and how he 'took' the island from him; and in phase four (lines 375–501), Miranda and Ferdinand meet.

The broad movement of the scene, and of each of its phases, resembling that of the play itself, is from despair to hope, from imprisonment to release, from death to life.

1. *art* magic.

2. *wild . . . roar* i.e. roused them to roaring like wild beasts.

2. *allay* soothe.

3–5. Miranda's description of the storm paints a picture of a war between sea and sky. Hot, black tar (stinking pitch) is about to be poured down like boiling oil from the castle walls of the sky on to the attacking waves below when the mountainous sea rises to swamp it. The welkin (sky) is described as having a cheek, i.e. the side of a grate of a fire or furnace, though cheek might also suggest cloud.

6. *brave* splendid.

7. *some noble creature* This is ironic as Miranda does not know that the ship has a king and his nobles on board.

8. *the cry* i.e. we split, we split: it knocked on the door of her heart.

13. *fraughting souls* cargo or freight of passengers and crew.

13. *Be collected* pull yourself together.

1–13. All four elements of matter which Prospero commands through the help of his 'spirits' – earth, water, air and fire – are mentioned.

14. *amazement* frenzy.

14. *piteous* compassionate.

15–21. References to family relationship occur very frequently in this scene (e.g. father, daughter, mother, brother, uncle, grandmother, sons).

20–1. *master . . . father* possessor of a very humble cell, and your equally lowly father.

22. *meddle* mingle.

Scene II

The island. Before Prospero's cell.

[Enter PROSPERO *and* MIRANDA*]*

Miranda

    If by your art, my dearest father, you have
    Put the wild waters in this roar, allay them.
    The sky, it seems, would pour down stinking pitch,
    But that the sea, mounting to th' welkin's cheek,
    Dashes the fire out. O, I have suffered   5
    With those that I saw suffer! A brave vessel,
    Who had no doubt some noble creature in her,
    Dash'd all to pieces! O, the cry did knock
    Against my very heart! Poor souls, they perish'd.
    Had I been any god of power, I would   10
    Have sunk the sea within the earth or ere
    It should the good ship so have swallow'd and
    The fraughting souls within her.

Prospero

                  Be collected;
    No more amazement; tell your piteous heart
    There's no harm done.

Miranda

           O, woe the day!

Prospero

                No harm.   15
    I have done nothing but in care of thee,
    Of thee, my dear one, thee, my daughter, who
    Art ignorant of what thou art, nought knowing
    Of whence I am, nor that I am more better
    Than Prospero, master of a full poor cell,   20
    And thy no greater father.

Miranda

             More to know
    Did never meddle with my thoughts.

Prospero

                'Tis time

25. *have comfort* let me reassure you.

27. *very virtue*, very heart of.
28. *provision* foresight (i.e. he has provided for it).

30. *perdition* loss.
31. *Betid* happened.
32. *Which* whom (i.e. which thou heard'st refers to creature and which thou saw'st to vessel).

35. *bootless inquisition* pointless questioning.
36–8. The audience's curiosity, like Miranda's, is aroused.

41. *Out* fully.
43–4. *Of . . . remembrance* describe any picture from the past that has lived in your memory.
44. *kept with* remained
44. *'Tis far off* the phrase suggests distance both in time and space, the remote past is suddenly becoming the present being brought near.
45–6. *And . . . warrants* more like a dream than a certainty guaranteed by my memory.
46–7. Miranda remembers waiting-women rather than her own mother, who seems to have died not long after Miranda was born. (See lines 68–9.)

I should inform thee farther. Lend thy hand,
And pluck my magic garment from me. So,

[Lays down his mantle]

Lie there my art. Wipe thou thine eyes, have comfort.   25
The direful spectacle of the wreck, which touch'd
The very virtue of compassion in thee,
I have with such provision in mine art
So safely ordered that there is no soul –
No, not so much perdition as an hair   30
Betid to any creature in the vessel
Which thou heard'st cry, which thou saw'st sink. Sit down,
For thou must now know farther.

Miranda
                You have often
Begun to tell me what I am, but stopp'd,
And left me to a bootless inquisition,   35
Concluding 'Stay, not yet'.

Prospero
             The hour's now come,
The very minute bids thee ope thine ear.
Obey, and be attentive. Canst thou remember
A time before we came unto this cell?
I do not think thou canst, for then thou wast not   40
Out three years old.

Miranda
         Certainly, sir, I can.

Prospero
By what? By any other house, or person?
Of any thing the image, tell me, that
Hath kept with thy remembrance?

Miranda
           'Tis far off,
And rather like a dream than an assurance   45
That my remembrance warrants. Had I not
Four, or five, women once, that tended me?

50. **dark . . . abysm** the deep, dim gulf of the past. The concrete term abyss together with backward suggests time in terms of space (i.e. Milan is far off in time and space).

53. This makes Miranda's age about fifteen, young by modern standards but physically mature enough in Shakespeare's day for marriage.

53. **since** ago.

55. **prince** sovereign ruler (rather than 'king's son').

56. **piece of virtue** perfect example of chastity.

59. **no worse issued** of equal birth; noble.

62. **heav'd**, expelled.

63. **holp** helped.

64–5. **To think . . . remembrance** when I think of the trouble I have made you recall in your mind, which I can no longer remember myself.

65. **farther** go on.

66–116. In these lines Prospero's bitter past experiences are emphasised.

67. **mark me** take careful note of what I say.

68. **perfidious** treacherous.

70. **manage of my state** management of my dukedom.

71. **signories** states (of Northern Italy).

71. **the first** the most eminent.

Prospero

 Thou hadst, and more, Miranda. But how is it
 That this lives in thy mind? What seest thou else
 In the dark backward and abysm of time?   50
 If thou rememb'rest aught, ere thou cam'st here,
 How thou cam'st here thou mayst.

Miranda

          But that I do not.

Prospero

 Twelve year since, Miranda, twelve year since,
 Thy father was the Duke of Milan, and
 A prince of power.

Miranda

       Sir, are not you my father?   55

Prospero

 Thy mother was a piece of virtue, and
 She said thou wast my daughter; and thy father
 Was Duke of Milan, and his only heir
 And princess no worse issued.

Miranda

         O, the heavens!
 What foul play had we that we came from thence? 60
 Or blessed was't we did?

Prospero

        Both, both, my girl.
 By foul play, as thou say'st, were we heav'd thence,
 But blessedly holp hither.

Miranda

        O, my heart bleeds
 To think o' th' teen that I have turn'd you to,
 Which is from my remembrance. Please you, farther. 65

Prospero

 My brother and thy uncle, call'd Antonio –
 I pray thee, mark me that a brother should
 Be so perfidious. He, whom next thyself
 Of all the world I lov'd, and to him put
 The manage of my state; as at that time   70
 Through all the signories it was the first,

72–3. *Prospero . . . dignity* Prospero, the principal Duke, holding that rank by virtue of his high reputation.

73. *liberal arts* intellectual studies. (The seven liberal arts were: grammar, logic, rhetoric, arithmetic, geometry, music and astronomy.)

75–7. *government . . . studies* the task of governing I placed upon my brother's shoulders and neglected my own public duties, increasingly carried away and absorbed by my private researches (i.e. into the hidden mysteries of nature and science).

77. *false* treacherous.

78. Prospero breaks up his long account of' 'the story so far' by repeatedly reminding Miranda to pay attention. This provides rests for actor and audience alike, and is made to seem natural as Miranda's attention wanders away to the supposed shipwreck.

79–87. *Being . . . out on't* Here, Prospero describes how his brother Antonio cunningly persuaded people at court to transfer their loyalty from Prospero to him. Once Antonio had gained control of officials and their departments, he was able to make everyone in the dukedom dance to whatever tune he chose to play: his stranglehold on power was like ivy on a royal oak, and it drained Prospero's authority.

81. *trash for over-topping* hold back a hound which outruns the pack, by attaching a weight or leash to its neck.

83. *key* from the image of a key used in turning a lock, Prospero moves rapidly in his heated imagination to a key in music.

89–93. *I thus . . . nature* my neglect of government and complete devotion to private study, and the development of my intellect with subjects which, except for being too remote from everyday realities, were worth far more than any ordinary person could appreciate, aroused the evil which was waiting in Antonio's character.

94–6. The image in parent and beget continues the references to family connections. Prospero says that his unlimited trust in his brother produced in Antonio a response which was equally as treacherous as Prospero's was trusting.

97–105. *He being . . . prerogative* Antonio, being placed in a position of lordly power, not only by the money coming from my estates but also from what my authority could demand in other ways, like someone who by repeating a lie makes his memory unable to distinguish the true from the false, really believed that he was the Duke, as a result of acting as my deputy and carrying out the public duties of the office with all its privileges.

And Prospero the prime duke, being so reputed
In dignity, and for the liberal arts
Without a parallel, those being all my study –
The government I cast upon my brother   75
And to my state grew stranger, being transported
And rapt in secret studies. Thy false uncle –
Dost thou attend me?

Miranda
                        Sir, most heedfully.

Prospero
Being once perfected how to grant suits,
How to deny them, who t' advance, and who   80
To trash for over-topping, new created
The creatures that were mine, I say, or chang'd 'em,
Or else new form'd 'em, having both the key
Of officer and office, set all hearts i' th' state
To what tune pleas'd his ear, that now he was   85
The ivy which had hid my princely trunk
And suck'd my verdure out on't. Thou attend'st not.

Miranda
O, good sir, I do!

Prospero
                        I pray thee, mark me.
I thus neglecting worldly ends, all dedicated
To closeness and the bettering of my mind   90
With that which, but by being so retir'd,
O'er-priz'd all popular rate, in my false brother
Awak'd an evil nature, and my trust,
Like a good parent, did beget of him
A falsehood, in its contrary as great   95
As my trust was, which had indeed no limit,
A confidence sans bound. He being thus lorded,
Not only with that my revenue yielded,
But what my power might else exact, like one
Who having into truth, by telling of it,   100
Made such a sinner of his memory,
To credit his own lie – he did believe
He was indeed the Duke; out o' th' substitution,

107–9. To have . . . Milan in order to have no barrier standing between him in his role as deputy and the reality of being Duke, he had to become the Duke of Milan himself, unconditionally.

110. temporal royalties state duties and functions as a ruler.

111. confederates allies.

112. So dry he was for sway so thirsty was he for power.

114. Subject . . . crown i.e. makes Antonio's lesser crown (coronet) owe allegiance to Alonso.

114–15. bend . . . unbow'd make Milan kneel (never having submitted to any state before) to Naples.

117. Mark . . . th'event note carefully the contract (made with Alonso) and what the outcome was.

118–20. I should . . . sons Miranda suggests that she would be breaking one of the Commandments (i.e. not honouring her father's mother) if she had anything less than the highest regard for her. Rather than think that Antonio was only a bastard-brother to her father, Miranda prefers to accept the fact that even the best families can produce 'black sheep' occasionally.

123–6. in lieu . . . dukedom according to the conditions agreed upon (the receiving of both homage and a great sum of tribute money) would in return at once throw me and my family out of our dukedom.

127–32. Whereon . . . crying self the economy of these lines shows Shakespeare at his most masterly: we can see the army which has been specially raised by Alonso waiting to crush any loyal opposition, hear the city clocks striking twelve; watch Antonio, perhaps there in person, drawing back the bolts of the great gates of Milan; and listen in the silence of the dead of night to the crying of the little child as the specially appointed agents, like evil spirits of midnight, hurry Prospero and his daughter away.

And executing th' outward face of royalty
With all prerogative. Hence his ambition growing – 105
Dost thou hear?

Miranda
             Your tale, sir, would cure deafness.

Prospero
To have no screen between this part he play'd
And him he play'd it for, he needs will be
Absolute Milan. Me, poor man – my library
Was dukedom large enough – of temporal royalties 110
He thinks me now incapable; confederates,
So dry he was for sway, wi' th' King of Naples,
To give him annual tribute, do him homage,
Subject his coronet to his crown, and bend
The dukedom, yet unbow'd – alas, poor Milan! – 115
To most ignoble stooping.

Miranda
             O the heavens!

Prospero
Mark his condition, and th' event, then tell me
If this might be a brother.

Miranda
             I should sin
To think but nobly of my grandmother:
Good wombs have borne bad sons.

Prospero
             Now the condition: 120
This King of Naples, being an enemy
To me inveterate, hearkens my brother's suit;
Which was, that he, in lieu o' th' premises,
Of homage, and I know not how much tribute,
Should presently extirpate me and mine 125
Out of the dukedom, and confer fair Milan
With all the honours on my brother. Whereon,
A treacherous army levied, one midnight
Fated to th' purpose, did Antonio open
The gates of Milan; and, i' th' dead of darkness, 130
The ministers for th' purpose hurried thence

134–5. *a hint . . . to't* an occasion which forces tears from my eyes.

136. *business* matter. The word is often used in the sense of intrigue or plot (e.g. line 142).

138. *impertinent* irrelevant.

139. *wench* lass (a term of affection, not only for a servant).

140. *provokes* raises.

140. *durst* dared.

141–2. *nor set/A mark so bloody* i.e. unlike staghunters who put the stag's blood on themselves at the kill.

143. *With . . . ends* with more pleasant colours (than blood-red) disguised their plans. (To 'paint' usually meant to cover up by using cosmetics as a disguise.)

144. *bark* ship (barque).

146. *carcass of a butt* skeleton of a tub, a small, leaky boat.

147. *tackle* ropes.

148. *hoist* placed.

149. *roar'd* though commonly used of lions and cannon, the word often meant 'loud lamentation' – that's to say 'weeping'.

151. *loving wrong* i.e. though sympathetic, the winds might have done them wrong by upsetting their little craft. (The phrase is an example of an oxymoron in which two seemingly-opposite ideas make sense.)

152. *cherubin* little angel.

154. *Infused* inspired.

155. *drops full salt* Prospero's bitter, stinging tears are as salty as the sea he is weeping into.

155. *deck'd* covered.

156–8. *which . . . ensue* your smile awakened my spirit, and encouraged me to endure whatever might follow.

Me and thy crying self.

Miranda

Alack, for pity!
I, not rememb'ring how I cried out then,
Will cry it o'er again; it is a hint
That wrings mine eyes to't.

Prospero

Hear a little further,   135
And then I'll bring thee to the present business
Which now's upon 's; without the which this story
Were most impertinent.

Miranda

Wherefore did they not
That hour destroy us?

Prospero

Well demanded, wench!
My tale provokes that question. Dear, they durst not,   140
So dear the love my people bore me, nor set
A mark so bloody on the business, but
With colours fairer painted their foul ends.
In few, they hurried us aboard a bark,
Bore us some leagues to sea, where they prepared   145
A rotten carcass of a butt, not rigg'd,
Nor tackle, sail, nor mast, the very rats
Instinctively have quit it. There they hoist us,
To cry to th' sea, that roar'd to us; to sigh
To th' winds, whose pity, sighing back again,   150
Did us but loving wrong.

Miranda

Alack, what trouble
Was I then to you!

Prospero

O, a cherubin
Thou wast that did preserve me! Thou didst smile,
Infused with a fortitude from heaven,
When I have deck'd the sea with drops full salt,   155
Under my burden groan'd; which rais'd in me
An undergoing stomach, to bear up

161. We hear Gonzalo's name for the first time.

162. *charity* kindness, love.

162–3. *appointed . . . design* put in charge of this plot.

164. *Rich garments* perhaps so that Prospero could maintain some dignity should he reach a place which had inhabitants. The same clothes are used in Act IV to distract Caliban and company, and in Act V to enable him to 'rise from the dead' and present himself as the rightful Duke.

164. *stuffs* materials, cloths.

165. *steaded* been very useful.

165. *gentleness* noble nature.

166. *furnish'd* equipped.

167. *volumes* Prospero's books containing magic learning.

168. *above* more highly than.

169. *Now I arise* i.e. to put on his magician's robe and charm Miranda asleep so that he can speak to his spirit-servant, Ariel. 'Arise' may also refer to his rising fortunes (see lines 178–9).

170. *Sit still* remain seated.

170. *the last* the conclusion.

171–4. *and here . . . careful* Prospero has been a better teacher than most princesses are lucky enough to get, and has taught her more than most princesses learn, who have more opportunities for distraction and less conscientious tutors. (The education of princes, i.e. rulers, was of great concern in the 16th and 17th centuries, and Shakespeare may be making a point of particular interest to the learned James I.)

177. *thus far forth* as far as this.

178–84. *By accident . . . droop* by an amazing chance, generous Mistress Fortune, now at last graciously smiling on me, has brought my enemies to our very shores, and by my foreknowledge I have discovered that reaching the summit of my fortunes depends upon a highly favourable star, whose astrological influence I must now woo, for if I fail to take this opportunity my fortunes will decline for ever from this moment.

Against what should ensue.

Miranda

How came we ashore?

Prospero

By Providence divine.
Some food we had and some fresh water that   160
A noble Neapolitan, Gonzalo,
Out of his charity, who being then appointed
Master of this design, did give us, with
Rich garments, linens, stuffs, and necessaries,
Which since have steaded much; so, of his gentleness,   165
Knowing I lov'd my books, he furnish'd me
From mine own library with volumes that
I prize above my dukedom.

Miranda

Would I might
But ever see that man!

Prospero

Now I arise.

[Puts on his mantle]

Sit still, and hear the last of our sea-sorrow.   170
Here in this island we arriv'd; and here
Have I, thy schoolmaster, made thee more profit
Than other princess' can, that have more time
For vainer hours, and tutors not so careful.

Miranda

Heavens thank you for't! And now, I pray you, sir,   175
For still 'tis beating in my mind, your reason
For raising this sea-storm?

Prospero

Know thus far forth:
By accident most strange, bountiful Fortune,
Now my dear lady, hath mine enemies
Brought to this shore, and by my prescience   180
I find my zenith doth depend upon
A most auspicious star, whose influence
If now I court not, but omit, my fortunes

185. *dullness* sleepiness.
186. *give it way* don't try to fight it.

187. *Come away servant* 'come here, my servant'.

Stage Direction. *Enter Ariel* In costume probably of sky-blue, in movement graceful and lively, Ariel, played in Shakespeare's day by a boy with an unbroken voice, personifies the speed of thought and the freedom of the imagination.

190. *answer thy best pleasure* 'obey your wishes fully and exactly'. Ariel is Prospero's agent: his highly active role is suggested not only by his physical movements, but by his language, which is full of verbs.

192–3. *To . . . quality* employ Ariel and all his fellow-spirits at your powerful command.

194. *Perform'd to point* in every detail.

195. *To every article* to the letter, in every respect.
196. *beak* pointed prow.
197. *waist* amidships.
197. *deck* poop-deck. (Ariel has gone from bow to stern, horizontally, before moving vertically, ascending from the rigging.)
198. *flam'd amazement* 'filling everyone with fear and wonder at my fiery appearance'.
200. *yards* yard-arms, on which the sails hang.
200. *distinctly* in several places at once.
201. *precursors* forerunners.
203. *fire and cracks* lightning and thunder.
204. *sulphurous roaring* also lightning and thunder.
204. *Neptune* god of the ocean.
206. *dread trident* Neptune's dreaded three-pronged spear, symbol of his power and majesty, shakes with fear.
207. *coil* uproar.
208. *infect* disturb.

Will ever after droop. Here cease more questions,
Thou art inclin'd to sleep; 'tis a good dullness, 185
And give it way. I know thou canst not choose.

[MIRANDA sleeps]

Come away, servant; come; I am ready now. Approach,
my Ariel. Come.

[Enter ARIEL]

Ariel
All hail, great master! grave sir, hail! I come
To answer thy best pleasure; be't to fly, 190
To swim, to dive into the fire, to ride
On the curl'd clouds. To thy strong bidding task
Ariel and all his quality.
Prospero
                Hast thou, spirit,
Perform'd to point the tempest that I bade thee?
Ariel
To every article. 195
I boarded the King's ship; now on the beak,
Now in the waist, the deck, in every cabin,
I flam'd amazement. Sometime I'd divide,
And burn in many places; on the topmast,
The yards, and bowsprit, would I flame distinctly, 200
Then meet and join. Jove's lightning, the precursors
O' th' dreadful thunder-claps, more momentary
And sight-outrunning were not; the fire and cracks
Of sulphurous roaring the most mighty Neptune
Seem to besiege, and make his bold waves tremble, 205
Yea, his dread trident shake.
Prospero
                My brave spirit!
Who was so firm, so constant, that this coil
Would not infect his reason?

208–10. *Not . . . desperation* there was not a person on board who did not feel the frenzy which madmen feel, or did not perform strange, even suicidal actions.

212. *Ferdinand* the audience now learns his name.

213. *up-staring* standing on end (with fear).

213. *like reeds* i.e. stiff with terror.

214. *Hell is empty* i.e. all the devils have left Hell to plague the ship.

218. *sustaining garments* clothes which kept them afloat or alive.

220. *troops* groups.

222. *cooling of the air* this suggests a hot day on which Ferdinand is cooling the air around him with his breath.

223. *odd angle* out-of-the-way corner.

224. *sad knot* to have folded arms *(knot)* was a sign of melancholy. Ferdinand believes he is the sole survivor of the wreck and is mourning his father's loss in particular. Ariel mischievously imitates *this*, his posture.

226. *in harbour* in a sheltered spot.

227. *deep nook* creek or inlet.

228. *midnight to fetch dew* dew for magical charms had to be gathered at midnight (the witching hour); the foul witch Sycorax also uses dew (for evil purposes), see line 321.

229. *still-vex'd Bermoothes* the Bermudas, constantly troubled by winds and storms. Shakespeare places Prospero's island, without any geographical precision, somewhere in the Mediterranean between Naples and Tunis.

231. *charm . . . labour* a spell added to the toil they have undergone.

Ariel
                          Not a soul
But felt a fever of the mad, and play'd
Some tricks of desperation. All but mariners   210
Plung'd in the foaming brine, and quit the vessel,
Then all afire with me; the King's son, Ferdinand,
With hair up-staring – then like reeds, not hair –
Was the first man that leapt; cried 'Hell is empty,
And all the devils are here.'
Prospero
                          Why, that's my spirit!   215
But was not this nigh shore?
Ariel
                          Close by, my master.

Prospero
But are they, Ariel, safe?
Ariel
                          Not a hair perish'd;
On their sustaining garments not a blemish,
But fresher than before; and, as thou bad'st me,
In troops I have dispers'd them 'bout the isle.   220
The King's son have I landed by himself,
Whom I left cooling of the air with sighs
In an odd angle of the isle, and sitting,
His arms in this sad knot.
Prospero
                          Of the King's ship,
The mariners, say how thou hast dispos'd,   225
And all the rest o' th' fleet?
Ariel
                          Safely in harbour
Is the King's ship; in the deep nook, where once
Thou call'dst me up at midnight to fetch dew
From the still-vex'd Bermoothes, there she's hid;
The mariners all under hatches stowed,   230
Who, with a charm join'd to their suffer'd labour,
I have left asleep; and for the rest o' th' fleet,
Which I dispers'd, they all have met again,

234. *flote* ocean-wave.

237. *great person* Alonso's royal self.

239. *mid season* noon.

240. *two glasses* two hours (measured by the hour-glass), i.e. it is now 2 p.m. The repeated references to time give the play its sense of urgency and inevitability.

241. *spent most preciously* i.e. they cannot afford to waste valuable time.

242–6. Magicians could control spirits only by continual effort, and Ariel's rebelliousness would be understood by Shakespeare's audience. Shakespeare uses the quarrel (which is only resolved at line 296) as a key way to introduce his next character, Caliban, before he appears.

242. *pains* work.

243. *remember* remind.

244. *moody* discontented.

246. *out* finished (i.e. time is up).

249. *grudge* complaining, murmuring.

250. *bate me* 'reduce my length of service by'.

252–6. Ariel's capacity to move through every element is again referred to.

252–3. *ooze . . . deep* ocean bed.

And are upon the Mediterranean flote
Bound sadly home for Naples, 235
Supposing that they saw the King's ship wreck'd,
And his great person perish.

Prospero

       Ariel, thy charge
Exactly is perform'd; but there's more work.
What is the time o' th' day?

Ariel

        Past the mid season.

Prospero

At least two glasses. The time 'twixt six and now 240
Must by us both be spent most preciously.

Ariel

Is there more toil? Since thou dost give me pains,
Let me remember thee what thou hast promis'd,
Which is not yet perform'd me.

Prospero

      How now, moody?
What is 't thou canst demand?

Ariel

       My liberty. 245

Prospero

Before the time be out? No more!

Ariel

        I prithee,
Remember I have done thee worthy service,
Told thee no lies, made thee no mistakings, serv'd
Without or grudge or grumblings. Thou didst promise
To bate me a full year.

Prospero

      Dost thou forget 250
From what a torment I did free thee?

Ariel

       No.

Prospero

Thou dost; and think'st it much to tread the ooze
Of the salt deep,

255–6. veins . . . frost in the subterranean streams which flow like veins through the earth's 'body' even when the surface is hardened by frost.

257. malignant rebellious.

258. Sycorax a name (found only in *The Tempest*) formed perhaps from a combination of the Greek *sys* (sow) and *korax* (raven) but also possibly deriving from *Coraxi*, the tribe from which the enchantress Circe came. (Circe was the sorceress in Homer's *Odyssey* who turned men into swine.)

261. Argier Algiers.

261. O was she so? Prospero's reply seems to be sarcastic, as if Ariel were mistaken, but he does not supply any alternative.

263. damn'd i.e. to hell. Sycorax and her *sorceries terrible* contrast with Prospero's 'good' magic. She was banished from Algiers for *mischiefs manifold* (countless crimes), whereas Prospero was exiled from Milan for the bettering of his mind (line 90). Further parallels and contrasts are that both are brought, in slightly different senses, to the island 'with child'; both are able to employ Ariel as a servant, both spend twelve years on the island. It is as if Shakespeare by means of these similarities is stressing the contrast between Prospero's white magic and Sycorax's black magic.

266–7. one thing . . . life this is unexplained, but may be that she was pregnant (line 269, *with child*).

269. blue-ey'd blue-lidded eyes, an indication of pregnancy.

272–3. spirit . . . commands because Ariel is a spirit of air he cannot carry out orders which are repellent to him since they come from a witch who works by means of the lowest element, earth. Her son, Caliban, is addressed as *thou earth* (line 314).

274. grand hests powerful commands.

275. potent ministers powerful spirits (of evil).

276. unmitigable incapable of being put off.

280. vent utter.

281. strike strike the water as they revolve.

To run upon the sharp wind of the north,
To do me business in the veins o' th' earth   255
When it is bak'd with frost.

Ariel

       I do not, sir.

Prospero

Thou liest, malignant thing. Hast thou forgot
The foul witch Sycorax, who with age and envy
Was grown into a hoop? Hast thou forgot her?

Ariel

No, sir.

Prospero

Thou hast. Where was she born? Speak, tell me.   260

Ariel

Sir, in Argier.

Prospero

      O, was she so? I must
Once in a month recount what thou hast been,
Which thou forget'st. This damn'd witch Sycorax,
For mischiefs manifold, and sorceries terrible
To enter human hearing, from Argier   265
Thou know'st was banish'd; for one thing she did
They would not take her life. Is not this true?

Ariel

Ay, sir.

Prospero

This blue-ey'd hag was hither brought with child,
And here was left by th' sailors. Thou, my slave,   270
As thou report'st thyself, wast then her servant,
And, for thou wast a spirit too delicate
To act her earthy and abhorr'd commands,
Refusing her grand hests, she did confine thee,
By help of her more potent ministers,   275
And in her most unmitigable rage,
Into a cloven pine; within which rift
Imprison'd thou didst painfully remain
A dozen years; within which space she died,
And left thee there, where thou didst vent thy groans 280

281–4. Then . . . shape Sycorax gave birth in animal fashion (*did Utter*) to a monster (a misshapen creature).

283. freckl'd spotted (perhaps like a venomous toad or snake). The handsome Ferdinand is a direct contrast physically and morally to Caliban.

284. Caliban the name is possibly a rough anagram of cannibal.

285. Dull slow-witted (in fact, just what Ariel is *not*).

287. groans the groans of Ariel as prisoner contrast with his songs when free.

288–9. wolves . . . bears seems strange on a Mediterranean island or in the Bahamas, but Prospero's island is imaginary rather then real. So moving were Ariel's agonized groans that even the most ferocious beasts felt sympathy.

291. again undo i.e. the decision having been made could not be reversed.

294. rend an oak (compare Act V, Scene i, line 45). an oak would be a stronger prison than a pine.

296. twelve winters i.e. your previous sentence will be repeated (only this time in an even more restrictive tree – an oak).

297–8. I will . . . gently I will obey your orders and perform my tasks as a spirit graciously.

301. nymph o' th' sea e.g. in Shakespeare's time, probably from a blue costume to a green one. Ariel is still, as at all times, invisible to everyone but Prospero, and his new appearance is both to delight the audience with a fresh vision of spectacular beauty and to remind them of the sea (particularly as he sings his sea songs to Ferdinand). His frequent changes of costume also echo the central theme of transformation in the play.

303. shape appearance, disguise.

304. diligence speed.

As fast as mill-wheels strike. Then was this island –
Save for the son that she did litter here,
A freckl'd whelp, hag-born – not honour'd with
A human shape.

Ariel

             Yes, Caliban her son.

Prospero

Dull thing, I say so; he, that Caliban   285
Whom now I keep in service. Thou best know'st
What torment I did find thee in; thy groans
Did make wolves howl, and penetrate the breasts
Of ever-angry bears; it was a torment
To lay upon the damn'd, which Sycorax   290
Could not again undo. It was mine art,
When I arriv'd and heard thee, that made gape
The pine, and let thee out.

Ariel

             I thank thee, master.

Prospero

If thou more murmur'st, I will rend an oak
And peg thee in his knotty entrails, till   295
Thou hast howl'd away twelve winters.

Ariel

             Pardon, master,
I will be correspondent to command,
And do my spriting gently.

Prospero

             Do so; and after two days
I will discharge thee.

Ariel

             That's my noble master!
What shall I do? Say what. What shall I do?   300

Prospero

Go make thyself like a nymph o' th' sea, be subject
To no sight but thine and mine, invisible
To every eyeball else. Go take this shape,
And hither come in 't. Go, hence with diligence!

[Exit ARIEL*]*

307. *Heaviness* sleepiness.

309. *villain* lowly servant.

311. *miss him* do without him.

312. *serves in offices* performs duties.

314. Caliban's den perhaps stands close to Prospero's cell, at the rear of the stage, like a dog-kennel *(here you sty me*, line 342).

314. *Thou earth* you clod.

316. *tortoise* i.e. slow-witted and cumbersome.

Stage Direction. *Re-enter Ariel* Ariel's change of costume was a simple one, taking only ten lines to complete. Both his appearance *(Fine apparition)* and his prompt and willing behaviour is in striking contrast to Caliban.

317. *quaint* handsome, elegant.

318. The whispered instruction (to fetch Ferdinand) arouses our curiosity and continues to show Prospero 'stage-managing' the events.

319–20. *got . . . dam* the Devil himself has possessed Sycorax and fathered Caliban.

321–4. *As wicked . . . all o'er* the poisonous dew collected by Sycorax contrasts with that collected by Ariel (line 228) and is appropriately gathered with a raven's feather (see note to line 258).The south-west wind was thought to bring fever, and some Elizabethan houses were built so that no windows faced south.

Awake, dear heart, awake; thou hast slept well;   305
    Awake.

Miranda

The strangeness of your story put
Heaviness in me.

Prospero

            Shake it off. Come on,
We'll visit Caliban, my slave, who never
Yields us kind answer.

Miranda

              'Tis a villain, sir,
I do not love to look on.

Prospero

              But as 'tis,   310
We cannot miss him: he does make our fire,
Fetch in our wood, and serves in offices
That profit us. What ho! slave! Caliban!
Thou earth, thou! Speak.

Caliban

[*Within*] There's wood enough within.

Prospero

Come forth, I say; there's other business for thee.   315
Come, thou tortoise! when?

    [Re-enter ARIEL *like a water-nymph]*

Fine apparition! My quaint Ariel,
Hark in thine ear.

Ariel

          My lord, it shall be done.

    [Exit]

Prospero

Thou poisonous slave, got by the devil himself
Upon thy wicked dam, come forth!   320

    [Enter CALIBAN*]*

Caliban

As wicked dew as e'er my mother brush'd

326. *pen they breath up* make you gasp for breath.

326. *pen* restrict.

326. *urchins* goblins in the shape of hedgehogs.

328–30. *thou . . . made 'em* Caliban will be nipped or stung so thick and fast that he will become riddled, like a honeycomb, every sting being more painful than any given by bees which make the cells.

329. *pinch* used several times in the play to suggest physical torture in which pincers are used.

330. *I must eat my dinner* Caliban, cowed for a moment, changes the subject and consoles himself with the thought of food.

331–2. *This . . . from me* To us, Prospero appears to have taken the island from Caliban, but 17th century thought might well have believed Prospero had a natural right to rule the inferior *deformed slave*.

333. *strok'st me* i.e. like a pet.

334. *berries* perhaps cedar-berries.

334–6. *teach . . . night* by using the words *the bigger light* and *the less*, rather than 'the sun' and 'the moon', Shakespeare gives us a glimpse of Caliban's actual lessons as he develops a vocabulary and also suggests a primitive awe, a sun and moon worship.

337. *qualities* natural properties, i.e. what the island had to offer.

338. In a single line of finely-patterned alliteration, Shakespeare conjures up a picture of the island, parts of which are life-giving (*springs* and *fertile*) and parts sterile (*brine-pits* and *barren place*).

339. *charms* spells.

340. *light* descend.

342. *sty me* pen me in (as in a pigsty).

345. *stripes* lashes, flogging.

345. *move* stir, make respond.

345. *us'd* treated.

346. *human* humane.

347–8. Caliban's attempted rape of Miranda contrasts strongly with the restrained behaviour of Ferdinand (see Act IV, Scene i, lines 23–31).

With raven's feather from unwholesome fen
Drop on you both! A south-west blow on ye
And blister you all o'er!

Prospero

For this, be sure, to-night thou shalt have cramps, 325
Side-stitches that shall pen thy breath up; urchins
Shall, for that vast of night that they may work,
All exercise on thee, thou shalt be pinch'd
As thick as honeycomb, each pinch more stinging
Than bees that made 'em.

Caliban

              I must eat my dinner. 330
This island's mine, by Sycorax my mother,
Which thou tak'st from me. When thou cam'st first,
Thou strok'st me and made much of me, wouldst
   give me
Water with berries in't, and teach me how
To name the bigger light, and how the less, 335
That burn by day and night; and then I lov'd thee,
And show'd thee all the qualities o' th' isle,
The fresh springs, brine-pits, barren place and fertile.
Curs'd be I that did so! All the charms
Of Sycorax, toads, beetles, bats, light on you! 340
For I am all the subjects that you have,
Which first was mine own king; and here you sty me
In this hard rock, whiles you do keep from me
The rest o' th' island.

Prospero

            Thou most lying slave,
Whom stripes may move, not kindness! I have us'd
   thee, 345
Filth as thou art, with human care, and lodg'd thee
In mine own cell, till thou didst seek to violate
The honour of my child.

Caliban

O ho, O ho! Would't had been done.
Thou didst prevent me; I had peopl'd else 350
This isle with Calibans.

351. *Abhorred* revolting.

352–3. *any print . . . all ill* Miranda cannot imprint on Caliban any idea of honourable behaviour because he is susceptible only to evil.

355–8. *When . . . known* when you were unable, in your primitive state, to put your thoughts into words, and could only express yourself in animal sounds, I gave you the gift of language so that you could communicate what you were thinking.

358. *thy vile race* your low nature, (*vile* is 'low-born' and *race* is 'inherited nature').

363. *profit on't* the best thing I have gained from it.

364. *red plague* the other two plague sores were the yellow and the black.

364. *rid* destroy.

365. *learning* teaching.

365. *Hag-seed* child of a witch.

366–7. *And . . . business* and you would be well advised to perform any other tasks promptly.

367. *Shrug'st thou* Caliban has made a gesture defiance.

367. *malice* malicious brute (i.e. creature with the power to harm, not merely spitefully-minded: see Act III, Scene ii, lines 83–7).

368. *thou neglect'st* you are negligent.

369. *rack* torture (put on the rack).

369. *old* of old people (e.g. arthritic pains).

373. *Setebos* 'the great devil Setebos' of the Patagonians (mentioned in Eden's *History of Travel*, 1577).

374. *vassal* slave.

Stage Direction. ***Re-enter Ariel*** Ariel accompanies his singing, probably on a lute. The irresistible power of music is seen for the first time in the play, and occurs again at frequent intervals. It is also the means by which Ariel moves the 'players' around to Prospero's commands.

Miranda
                              Abhorred slave,
Which any print of goodness wilt not take,
Being capable of all ill! I pitied thee,
Took pains to make thee speak, taught thee each hour
One thing or other. When thou didst not, savage,   355
Know thine own meaning, but wouldst gabble like
A thing most brutish, I endow'd thy purposes
With words that made them known. But thy vile race,
Though thou didst learn, had that in't which good
     natures
Could not abide to be with; therefore wast thou   360
Deservedly confin'd into this rock, who hadst
Deserv'd more than a prison.

Caliban
You taught me language, and my profit on't
Is, I know how to curse. The red plague rid you
For learning me your language!

Prospero
                              Hag-seed, hence!   365
Fetch us in fuel. And be quick, thou 'rt best,
To answer other business. Shrug'st thou, malice?
If thou neglect'st, or dost unwillingly
What I command, I'll rack thee with old cramps,
Fill all thy bones with aches, make thee roar,   370
That beasts shall tremble at thy din.

Caliban
                              No, pray thee.
[Aside] I must obey. His art is of such pow'r,
It would control my dam's god, Setebos,
And make a vassal of him.

Prospero
                    So, slave, hence!

[Exit CALIBAN*]*

[Re-enter ARIEL *invisible, playing and singing;*
FERDINAND *following]*

43

375–80. Ariel's song calls his fellow spirits to:

(a) come to the golden beaches of the island (375) as if to a great hall in which they will dance,

(b) *take hands* (376) to begin their ceremonious dance, and when they have

(c) *curtsied* (377), i.e. 'done courtesy' by bowing to each other and kissed the waves, which are still in uproar from the tempest, into silence *(whist)* in lines 377–8,

(d) dance, *foot it*, gracefully, *featly*, (379) and also

(e) accompany his song by singing a refrain, *burden* to it (380).

381–6. The *bow-wow* may refer to sounds made at ceremonial dances of the time, and perhaps the *watch-dogs* and *strutting chanticleer* suggest the arrival of dawn when spirits released at midnight to visit the world were forced to return to the underworld.

388. Where . . . earth? the *burden* has been sung *dispersedly*, i.e. from various parts of the stage.

389. waits upon attends. A god or goddess would be accompanied by the divine power of music. Miranda is taken for a goddess (line 422) by Ferdinand, and Prospero is virtually *god o'th' island*.

391. again, repeatedly.

391. wreck shipwrecking.

392. crept by me moved slowly and stealthily past me.

393. Allaying soothing.

393. passion, passionate sorrow.

394. Air tune.

397–405. Ariel's song to Ferdinand confirms his fears that his father is dead, by telling him that he is lying in thirty feet of water. However, he also tries to help him through this unwelcome news by saying that he (the King) is undergoing a physical transformation. This will be different from the usual processes of decay: this *sea-change* will make his father a precious object (of *coral* and *pearl*) rather than just 'dust'. Alonso's transformation into *something rich and strange* is to be a spiritual one rather than simply a physical one.

403. hourly ring his knell ring his funeral bell every hour, as fits with the death of a king.

404. This dirge-like *burden* contrasts with the lively sounds of the watchdogs and cock.

[ARIEL'S *Song*]

Come unto these yellow sands, 375
    And then take hands;
Curtsied when you have and kiss'd,
    The wild waves whist,
Foot it featly here and there,
    And, sweet sprites, the burden bear. 380
Hark, hark!
    Burden dispersedly. Bow-wow.
The watch dogs bark.
    Burden dispersedly. Bow-wow.
Hark, hark! I hear 385
    The strain of strutting chanticleer
Cry, Cock-a-diddle-dow.

Ferdinand

Where should this music be? I' th' air or th' earth?
It sounds no more; and sure it waits upon
Some god o' th' island. Sitting on a bank, 390
Weeping again the King my father's wreck,
This music crept by me upon the waters,
Allaying both their fury and my passion
With its sweet air; thence I have follow'd it,
Or it hath drawn me rather. But 'tis gone. 395
No, it begins again.

[ARIEL'S *Song*]

Full fathom five thy father lies;
    Of his bones are coral made;
Those are pearls that were his eyes;
    Nothing of him that doth fade 400
But doth suffer a sea-change
Into something rich and strange.
Sea-nymphs hourly ring his knell:
Burden. Ding-dong.
Hark! now I hear them – Ding-dong bell. 405

406. *The ditty . . . father* the words of this song commemorate my father's death by drowning.

407–8. *mortal business* (this singing is no) human matter.

407–8. *owes* owns, possesses.

409–10. *The fringed . . . yond* Prospero tells Miranda to raise *(advance)* her eyes *(fringed curtains* are literally her eyelids with their eyelashes) and tell him what she sees over there *(yond)*.

412. *brave form* noble appearance. Perhaps there is a note of disappointment in *But 'tis a spirit*.

415–16. Prospero uses the image of staining: Ferdinand's salt tears have affected his appearance (whereas the salt sea has not stained his or the courtiers' garments), and also the image of a worm *(canker)* eating into a beautiful bud or petal (i.e. his cheek).

417. *fellows* companions, associates.

419. *natural* belonging to nature (i.e. not spiritual).

420–21. *It . . . prompts it* Ferdinand and Miranda are free to make their own minds up and Prospero can only 'prompt' them by arranging that they meet. He is delighted to see that his plan is working. *(It goes on.)*

422. *goddess* the lovers' responses to each other continue to be identical. To him, she is a *goddess; to* her, he is a *thing divine*.

423. *airs* musical sounds, melodies, songs (compare line 394).

423–4. *Vouchsafe . . . know* grant my request to know.

424. *remain* dwell.

425. *good instruction* helpful information.

426. *bear me* conduct myself, behave.

426–8. Ferdinand's most important question *(prime request)*, given added weight by coming at the end of the speech, is whether or not Miranda is a *maid* (i.e. a mortal girl, not an immortal goddess). By calling her *wonder* he is, without knowing it, paraphrasing her name, Miranda.

429. *a maid* (a) a maiden, i.e. unmarried, (b) a virgin.

Ferdinand
    The ditty does remember my drown'd father.
    This is no mortal business, nor no sound
    That the earth owes. I hear it now above me.
Prospero
    The fringed curtains of thine eye advance,
    And say what thou seest yond.
Miranda

                  What is't? a spirit?   410
    Lord, how it looks about! Believe me, sir,
    It carries a brave form. But 'tis a spirit.
Prospero
    No, wench, it eats and sleeps and hath such senses
    As we have, such. This gallant which thou seest
    Was in the wreck; and but he's something stain'd   415
    With grief, that's beauty's canker, thou mightst call
       him
    A goodly person. He hath lost his fellows,
    And strays about to find 'em.
Miranda

                  I might call him
    A thing divine; for nothing natural
    I ever saw so noble.
Prospero
    [Aside]   It goes on, I see,   420
    As my soul prompts it. Spirit, fine spirit! I'll free thee
    Within two days for this.
Ferdinand

               Most sure, the goddess
    On whom these airs attend! Vouchsafe my pray'r
    May know if you remain upon this island;
    And that you will some good instruction give   425
    How I may bear me here. My prime request,
    Which I do last pronounce, is, O you wonder!
    If you be maid or no?
Miranda

             No wonder, sir;
    But certainly a maid.

430. *this speech* this language.

431. *Were I but where 'tis spoken* the sense of being on a remote island, both in time and place, is increased by constant references to the distant world across the sea.

431. *the best?* i.e. the King?

433. *single* alone and helpless.

433. *wonders* is amazed.

434. *He does hear me* Ferdinand is saying that since he is now the King of Naples, and can hear himself speaking, it follows that the King of Naples does hear him.

436. *mine eyes . . . ebb* Ferdinand uses a sea-image to describe his weeping. His eyes have been at high tide, flooded with tears ever since he saw his father drowned.

438. *Duke of Milan* i.e. Antonio. Just as Ferdinand is unaware he isn't yet King of Naples (because his father is still alive), so is he also unaware that Antonio is *not* the Duke of Milan (because Prospero is still alive). These are good examples of dramatic irony.

439. *his brave son* 'his excellent son'. We hear nothing more of Antonio having a son; perhaps he was sailing in one of the other vessels in the fleet (now *bound sadly for Naples)* and is presumed lost by Ferdinand.

440. *more braver* the use of a double comparative is quite common in Shakespeare.

440. *control* contradict.

442. *chang'd eyes* literally 'exchanged eyes' from gazing so magnetically at each other in their 'love at first sight' meeting. Is this rather like exchanging love-tokens (i.e rings, flowers etc)?

444–5. Prospero is 'playing the strict father' and speaking with irony. He speaks *ungently,* i.e. harshly.

444. *done yourself some wrong* made a mistake.

448. *To be inclin'd my way* i.e. may compassion urge my father to bend in my direction, sympathize with my feelings.

449. *affection not gone forth* if you haven't given your heart to anyone already.

450. *Soft, sir* just a moment, not so fast.

451–3. *but this . . . light* but I must make the rapid development of their feelings towards one another less easy, in case by winning each other too easily they do not value each other highly enough.

Ferdinand

                   My language? Heavens!
I am the best of them that speak this speech,   430
Were I but where 'tis spoken.

Prospero

                      How? the best?
What wert thou, if the King of Naples heard thee?

Ferdinand

A single thing, as I am now, that wonders
To hear thee speak of Naples. He does hear me;
And that he does I weep. Myself am Naples,   435
Who with mine eyes, never since at ebb, beheld
The King my father wreck'd.

Miranda

                  Alack, for mercy!

Ferdinand

Yes, faith, and all his lords, the Duke of Milan
And his brave son being twain.

Prospero

[Aside]   The Duke of Milan
And his more braver daughter could control thee,   440
If now 'twere fit to do't. At the first sight
They have chang'd eyes. Delicate Ariel,
I'll set thee free for this. *[To* FERDINAND*]* A word,
   good sir;
I fear you have done yourself some wrong; a word.

Miranda

Why speaks my father so ungently? This   445
Is the third man that e'er I saw; the first
That e'er I sigh'd for. Pity move my father
To be inclin'd my way!

Ferdinand

              O, if a virgin,
And your affection not gone forth, I'll make you
The Queen of Naples.

Prospero

            Soft, sir! one word more.   450
[Aside] They are both in cither's pow'rs; but this swift
  business

454. *attend* listen to, pay attention to.

454. *usurp* assume, take.

454. *ow'st not* do not own, is not rightly yours. (Prospero is accusing Ferdinand of committing the same sins as the older generation.)

458–60. Miranda is here expressing the idea, popular in the thought of Shakespeare's time, that (a) anyone with who looks as handsome as Ferdinand does on the outside must be spiritually good, (b) even if the Devil (evil) did live inside such a body *(temple)*, Good would nevertheless do all it could to live there as well (i.e. in its rightful dwelling place). And so, because Good and Evil cannot exist together, Evil would be driven out of such a handsome body.

461. *a traitor* treacherous.

462–5. *manacle etc* to test Ferdinand's manhood, Prospero threatens to treat him as a mutinous common sailor rather than as a prince.

466. *such entertainment* such treatment, such a reception.

468–9. *Make not . . . fearful* don't judge him too hastily; he's of noble birth and breeding, and no coward (i.e. he will naturally resist by drawing his sword).

470. *My foot my tutor?* i.e. 'Are you, my inferior, telling me what to do?' (This rebuke would look even more vivid if Miranda is on her knees at his feet.)

470. *Put thy sword up* sheathe your sword.

472. *possess'd* seized.

472. *thy ward* your 'on guard' position.

473–4. *For . . . drop* Ferdinand's sword is still drawn, and Prospero probably says what he can do rather than does it.

I must uneasy make, lest too light winning
Make the prize light. *[To* FERDINAND*]* One word
   more; I charge thee
That thou attend me; thou dost here usurp
The name thou ow'st not; and hast put thyself   455
Upon this island as a spy, to win it
From me, the lord on't.

Ferdinand

                         No, as I am a man.

Miranda

There's nothing ill can dwell in such a temple.
If the ill spirit have so fair a house,
Good things will strive to dwell with't.

Prospero

                                   Follow me.   460

Speak not you for him; he's a traitor. Come;
I'll manacle thy neck and feet together.
Sea-water shalt thou drink; thy food shall be
The fresh-brook mussels, wither'd roots, and husks
Wherein the acorn cradled. Follow.

Ferdinand

                              No;   465

I will resist such entertainment till
Mine enemy has more power.

                [He draws, and is charmed from moving]

Miranda

                         O dear father,
Make not too rash a trial of him, for
He's gentle, and not fearful.

Prospero

                         What, I say,
My foot my tutor? Put thy sword up, traitor;   470
Who mak'st a show but dar'st not strike, thy
   conscience
Is so possess'd with guilt. Come from thy ward;
For I can here disarm thee with this stick
And make thy weapon drop.

475–82. Ferdinand has been tested by Prospero and shown himself so far to be strong-willed. Miranda's feelings are now being tested too by Prospero's apparent spite towards Ferdinand, and at the same time are being strengthened.

476. *surety* security, bail.

478. *advocate for an impostor* a lawyer to defend a traitor.

480. *To th' most of men* compared with the majority of men.

482. *affections* wishes.

484. *obey* perhaps it is at this moment that Ferdinand sheathes his sword.

485–6. *Thy nerves . . . in them* 'your sinews are as weak as when you were an infant, and have no strength in them' (i.e. to wield a sword).

487. *My spirits . . . bound up* Ferdinand describes the feeling of helplessness experienced in dreams, when one is unable to perform some action (e.g. running away). In *bound up* there is another example of binding before later release.

490. *subdu'd*, controlled.

490. *light* trivial.

491. *through my prison* from my prison window.

492–4. *All corners . . . prison* let those who are free make use of the rest of the world, to its remotest extremities; I shall need no more room than my prison provides.

494. *It works* i.e. my plan. Whatever Prospero does to discourage Ferdinand only serves to increase his devotion, as Prospero hoped it would.

Miranda

                           Beseech you, father!

Prospero

   Hence! Hang not on my garments.

Miranda

                       Sir, have pity;   475

   I'll be his surety.

Prospero

                Silence! One word more
Shall make me chide thee, if not hate thee. What!
An advocate for an impostor! hush!
Thou think'st there is no more such shapes as he,
Having seen but him and Caliban. Foolish wench!   480
To th' most of men this is a Caliban,
And they to him are angels.

Miranda

                   My affections
Are then most humble; I have no ambition
To see a goodlier man.

Prospero

                Come on; obey.
Thy nerves are in their infancy again,   485
And have no vigour in them.

Ferdinand

                   So they are;
My spirits, as in a dream, are all bound up.
My father's loss, the weakness which I feel,
The wreck of all my friends, nor this man's threats
To whom I am subdu'd, are but light to me,   490
Might I but through my prison once a day
Behold this maid. All corners else o' th' earth
Let liberty make use of; space enough
Have I in such a prison.

Prospero

   [Aside]   It works. *[To* FERDINAND*]* Come on. –
Thou hast done well, fine Ariel! *[To* FERDINAND*]*
   Follow me.   495
   [To ARIEL*]* Hark what thou else shalt do me.

498. *unwonted* unusual

501. *points* smallest details.

501. *to th' syllable* exactly, to the letter.

502. *Speak not for him* don't try to plead for him.

By the end of Act I the introductory phase of the play is complete: characters, general situation (i.e. the tempest and what has led to it), setting and themes have all been established. Prospero, who dominates Act I, now retires into the background to allow three particular situations to develop, before moving into the foreground again in Acts IV and V. The three situations are:

- the Ferdinand–Miranda love story
- the plot by Sebastian and Antonio to murder Alonso
- the parallel plot by Caliban, Stephano and Trinculo to murder Prospero.

The first of these situations has already developed by the end of Act I and reaches its climax when Ferdinand and Miranda next appear in Act III, Scene i, at the turning point of the play.

Miranda
                                                    Be of comfort;
My father's of a better nature, sir,
Than he appears by speech; this is unwonted
Which now came from him.

Prospero
    [To ARIEL]   Thou shalt be as free
As mountain winds; but then exactly do   500
All points of my command.

Ariel
                            To th' syllable.

Prospero
    [To FERDINAND] Come, follow.
            [To MIRANDA] Speak not for him.

            [Exeunt]

ACT II, SCENE I

In this scene the characters of Alonso, Gonzalo, Sebastian, and Antonio, all briefly sketched in Act I, scene i, are more fully revealed. Gonzalo's loyal attempts to cheer Alonso up in the face of Sebastian and Antonio's cold and cynical comments, make up the first half of the scene, while Sebastian and Antonio's murderous plotting fill the second half. Prospero's island provides a 'test bed' for each character, on which strengths and weaknesses in personality are revealed. Gonzalo, for instance, unlike his master, Alonso, resists the temptation to despair; but Sebastian and Antonio do not resist the temptation offered by the sleeping bodies of the king and his chief counsellor.

Stage Direction. Another part: on the island there is little clear sense of location other than at Prospero's cell, and little if any scenery would have been necessary in the original production – a few property rocks and bushes at the most. *and others:* nowadays most productions of the play limit Alonso's party to those named, who provide enough for a group but not enough to clutter the stage.

3–4. *hint of woe/Is common* this sad occasion is a common enough one.

5–6. *The masters . . . woe* the owners of some merchant vessel, and the merchant himself, have precisely the same reason to be sad, (i.e. the sailor's wife awaits the return of her husband; the ship's owners, their ship; and the trader, his cargo).

8–9. *weigh . . . comfort* let the consolation of having survived outweigh (be balanced against) our reason for grief.

10–181. Sebastian and Antonio might be sitting or standing together apart from the others, on the opposite side of the stage from Alonso and Gonzalo. Gonzalo may be in the centre, and have to turn towards Sebastian and Antonio and away from the king to answer their unpleasant remarks.

9–10. *peace . . . porridge* the first of many poor puns, this one plays on *peace* and *pease*, an ingredient in porridge.

11. *visitor . . . o'er so* the parish visitor (charitably bringing cold porridge to the sick) will not give up comforting him as easily (as the sick man gives up hope, or being comforted).

12. *wit* mind, intelligence.

13. *strike* referring to a striking or chiming watch, this suggests that Gonzalo is trying to get Alonso's attention.

15. *One – Tell* one chime has sounded – count the others.

16–17. *When . . . entertainer* if every sorrow that is presented to a person is accepted by him, then that person receives . . .

18. *dollar* i.e. payment for entertainment (hospitality), a *dollar* could mean 'thaler' (a German coin) or a 'piece of eight' (a Spanish coin).

ACT TWO

Scene I

Another part of the island.

[*Enter* ALONSO, SEBASTIAN, ANTONIO, GONZALO,
ADRIAN, FRANCISCO, *and others*]

Gonzalo
Beseech you, sir, be merry, you have cause,
So have we all, of joy; for our escape
Is much beyond our loss. Our hint of woe
Is common; every day, some sailor's wife,
The masters of some merchant, and the merchant,   5
Have just our theme of woe; but for the miracle,
I mean our preservation, few in millions
Can speak like us. Then wisely, good sir, weigh
Our sorrow with our comfort.

Alonso
                                        Prithee, peace.

Sebastian
He receives comfort like cold porridge.   10

Antonio
The visitor will not give him o'er so.

Sebastian
Look, he's winding up the watch of his wit; by and by
it will strike.

Gonzalo
Sir –

Sebastian
One – Tell.   15

Gonzalo
When every grief is entertain'd that's offer'd,
Comes to th' entertainer –

Sebastian
A dollar.

19–21. *Dolour . . . should* Gonzalo turns away from Alonso for a moment to hit back with his pun on *dollar – dolour* (grief) and Sebastian is reduced to a sulky and ineffective reply.

23. *spendthrift* further clever use of language related to dollar (coin), perhaps, trying to score off Gonzalo again (Gonzalo having turned back to address Alonso with *Therefore, my lord –*).

29. *The old cock* i.e. Gonzalo.

32. *A laughter* i.e. whoever loses will pay by laughing.

33. *A match!* done! Agreed!

35–6. *Ha, ha, ha/So you're paid* perhaps Antonio laughs naturally, simply because he has won the bet, and Sebastian says that by laughing Antonio has paid Sebastian's debt for him.

Gonzalo
  Dolour conies to him, indeed, you have spoken
  truer than you purpos'd.   20
Sebastian
  You have taken it wiselier than I meant you should.
Gonzalo
  Therefore, my lord –
Antonio
  Fie, what a spendthrift is he of his tongue!
Alonso
  I prithee, spare.
Gonzalo
  Well, I have done; but yet –   25
Sebastian
  He will be talking.
Antonio
  Which, of he or Adrian, for a good wager, first begins
  to crow?
Sebastian
  The old cock.
Antonio
  The cock'rel.   30
Sebastian
  Done. The wager?
Antonio
  A laughter.
Sebastian
  A match!
Adrian
  Though this island seem to be desert –
Antonio
  Ha, ha, ha!   35
Sebastian
  So, you're paid.
Adrian
  Uninhabitable, and almost inaccessible –
Sebastian
  Yet –

40. *He could not miss't* (a) do without it (i.e. the island, or he would be in the sea), (b) miss saying it (the *word yet*).

41–2. *subtle . . . temperance* mild and pleasant climate.

43. *Temperance was a delicate wench* Antonio perhaps hints that Temperance

(moderation), a Puritan girl's name, was 'delicate' in a rude rather than a pure sense.

44. *subtle* this time meaning crafty or cunning in an mocking way.

44. *learnedly deliver'd* perhaps the studious (?) Adrian *(cock'rel* to the *old cock,*), in using long words and speaking to them deliberately, is seen as a future Gonzalo.

52. *tawny* yellow-brown. Sebastian takes a cynical view of the land and situation, and is not prepared to see anything good about it.

54–5. *He misses . . . totally* Antonio perhaps means that Gonzalo sees every detail, and Sebastian replies that 'he can't see the wood for the trees' (he 'miss-takes' the truth).

56. *rarity* marvel.

57. *credit* belief.

58. *vouch'd* claimed as true (by travellers).

Adrian
Yet –
Antonio
He could not miss't.   40
Adrian
It must needs be of subtle, tender, and delicate temperance.
Antonio
Temperance was a delicate wench.
Sebastian
Ay, and a subtle; as he most learnedly deliver'd.
Adrian
The air breathes upon us here most sweetly.   45
Sebastian
As if it had lungs, and rotten ones.
Antonio
Or, as 'twere perfum'd by a fen.
Gonzalo
Here is everything advantageous to life.
Antonio
True, save means to live.
Sebastian
Of that there's none, or little.   50
Gonzalo
How lush and lusty the grass looks! how green!
Antonio
The ground indeed is tawny.
Sebastian
With an eye of green in't.
Antonio
He misses not much.
Sebastian
No, he doth but mistake the truth totally.   55
Gonzalo
But the rarity of it is, which is indeed almost beyond credit –
Sebastian
As many vouch'd rarities are.

61. *glosses* glossiness, shining newness.

63–4. *If but . . . lies?* perhaps Antonio is saying that on the outside their garments may seem as good as new, but that the truth is to be found beneath the surface (i.e. by examining a pocket). He won't be taken in by appearances, though in this case the appearance *is* (miraculously) the reality, but his cynicism prevents him from seeing it.

65. *pocket up* hide away, conceal.

67. *at the marriage* the audience is given the reason for the sea voyage.

69–70. *'Twas . . . return* Sebastian is being sarcastic in his reference to a *sweet marriage;* and perhaps there is a dramatic irony in his use of *prosper* (i.e. not realising that Prospero is on the island).

71. *such a paragon to* such a perfect model for.

73–81. This passage is rather complicated, but becomes less so if we realize that there are *two* stories about Dido, Queen of Carthage. In the first, from Virgil's *Aeneid*, she became the lover of Aeneas. In the second, from a story by Boccaccio she refused a succession of suitors. In both stories she is a widow, and in both she cremates herself: in the first, because Aeneas abandons her, and in the second to avoid being forced into a second marriage (thus proving her faithfulness to her dead husband). Antonio is thinking of Virgil's version and Gonzalo of Boccaccio's story. As far as Antonio is concerned Dido is an unfaithful widow, false to her husband's memory, but for Gonzalo she is a model of decency.

80–2. Gonzalo mistakenly thinks that Tunis stands on the site of Carthage (whereas the ruins of the ancient city stand not far from Tunis), and Antonio scornfully says that he, Gonzalo, has raised a whole city and not (as Amphion did with his harp) only the walls (of Thebes).

Gonzalo

That our garments, being, as they were, drench'd in the sea, hold, notwithstanding, their freshness and glosses, being rather new-dy'd, than stain'd with salt water. 60

Antonio

If but one of his pockets could speak, would it not say he lies?

Sebastian

Ay, or very falsely pocket up his report. 65

Gonzalo

Methinks our garments are now as fresh as when we put them on first in Afric, at the marriage of the King's fair daughter Claribel to the King of Tunis.

Sebastian

'Twas a sweet marriage, and we prosper well in our return. 70

Adrian

Tunis was never grac'd before with such a paragon to their queen.

Gonzalo

Not since widow Dido's time.

Antonio

Widow! a pox o' that! How came that 'widow' in? Widow Dido! 75

Sebastian

What if he had said 'widower Æneas' too? Good Lord, how you take it!

Adrian

'Widow Dido' said you? You make me study of that. She was of Carthage, not of Tunis.

Gonzalo

This Tunis, sir, was Carthage. 80

Adrian

Carthage?

Gonzalo

I assure you, Carthage.

85. *What . . . next?* further dramatic irony: Antonio little realizes that although Gonzalo may not be a magician, Prospero is already making an *impossible matter* easy.

90. *Ay* Gonzalo is probably speaking with Adrian during lines 81–7, following an earlier conversation between them, and Antonio takes it that he is agreeing to the comic exaggerations about islands and apples.
91. *in good time* at last! (i.e. at last Gonzalo has responded).

95. *And . . . there* a mocking echo of line 69.

96. *Bate . . . Dido* with the exception of widow Dido, please.

97. *O . . . Ay . . . Dido* some rhyme effect is suggested here, e.g. 'widow Dido'.
98. *doublet* close-fitting garment, with or without sleeves, worn as a tunic over a shirt and under a longer outer garment or short cloak.
99. *in a sort* more or less, after a fashion.
100. *That . . . fish'd for* you took your time to land that fish, i.e. to make that statement (that your doublet was only more or less as fresh as when you first wore it). Gonzalo *first wore* it at the wedding presumably because it had been specially made for the royal wedding.

102–3. *You cram . . . sense* Alonso is sick of being reminded of the wedding, the result of which is that he has lost both his children. The image is of force-feeding: as his hearing *(sense)* is crammed with words that sickened him.
105. *rate* judgement.

Antonio
　His word is more than the miraculous harp.
Sebastian
　He hath rais'd the wall, and houses too.
Antonio
　What impossible matter will he make easy next?　85
Sebastian
　I think he will carry this island home in his pocket,
　and give it his son for an apple.
Antonio
　And, sowing the kernels of it in the sea, bring forth
　more islands.
Gonzalo
　Ay.　90
Antonio
　Why, in good time.
Gonzalo
　Sir, we were talking that our garments seem now as
　fresh as when we were at Tunis at the marriage of your
　daughter, who is now Queen.
Antonio
　And the rarest that e'er came there.　95
Sebastian
　Bate, I beseech you, widow Dido.
Antonio
　O, widow Dido! Ay, widow Dido.
Gonzalo
　Is not, sir, my doublet as fresh as the first day I wore
　it? I mean, in a sort.
Antonio
　That 'sort' was well fish'd for.　100
Gonzalo
　When I wore it at your daughter's marriage?
Alonso
　You cram these words into mine ears against
　The stomach of my sense. Would I had never
　Married my daughter there, for, coming thence,
　My son is lost, and, in my rate, she too,　105

107–8. *O thou . . . Milan* presumably as part of the deal with Alonso, Antonio has agreed to Ferdinand (rather than his own son) inheriting the Dukedom of Milan. It is ironic that Ferdinand, in marrying Miranda, will in fact rule *both* Naples and Milan.

108. *strange* foreign.

109–18. This is Francisco's only speech in the play – he gives an heroic picture of Ferdinand battling his way ashore.

109–18. *beat, ride, trod, enmity, bold, lusty stroke* all give an impression of a champion in battle, in single fight against a whole army.

109–18. *surge most swoln* mountainous wave (like an advancing rank of soldiers).

109–18. *contentious waves* challenging waves (of troops).

116–117. *To th' shore . . . him* the overhanging cliffs (or perhaps concave sand-dunes) are pictured as leaning to help him ashore.

116. *his* its.

116. *basis* foot (i.e. beach). The image may continue the battle idea: the land (Ferdinand's ally) is like a friendly soldier coming to the aid of the hero struck down in the fight.

119–21. *loss . . . bless . . . lose* the verbs gain emphasis from the '1' and 's' alliterations. *Lose* repeats *loss,* but is also *loose* (release), a term used to describe the releasing of a mare to mate with a stallion, and would express Sebastian's disgust at Alonso's allowing the *fair soul* (line 125) to marry a dark-skinned African.

122–3. *Where . . . on't* where (i.e. in Africa) she, to say the least, is banished from you (i.e. like a traitor rather than your loving daugher), who have good reason to weep over your grievous loss.

126. *Weigh'd . . . obedience* (undecided) whether to refuse *(loathness:* reluctance) or to obey.

127. *Which . . . bow* which end of the scales should descend (i.e. which side to come down on, either not to marry the African or to obey her father).

129. *Moe* more.

129. *of this business' making* as the result of this wedding. (Sebastian's bitter use of *business* suggests a purely political marriage.)

130. *Than . . . them* Sebastian assumes that the whole fleet has been lost and that he and his companions are the sole survivors.

131. *So is . . . loss* so is the keenest feeling of loss.

Who is so far from Italy removed
I ne'er again shall see her. O thou mine heir
Of Naples and of Milan, what strange fish
Hath made his meal on thee?

Francisco

                    Sir, he may live;
I saw him beat the surges under him,   110
And ride upon their backs, he trod the water,
Whose enmity he flung aside, and breasted
The surge most swoln that met him, his bold head
'Bove the contentious waves he kept, and oared
Himself with his good arms in lusty stroke   115
To th' shore, that o'er his wave-worn basis bowed,
As stooping to relieve him. I not doubt
He came alive to land.

Alonso

               No, no, he's gone.

Sebastian

Sir, you may thank yourself for this great loss,
That would not bless our Europe with your daughter, 120
But rather lose her to an African;
Where she, at least, is banish'd from your eye,
Who hath cause to wet the grief on't.

Alonso

                     Prithee, peace.

Sebastian

You were kneel'd to, and importun'd otherwise
By all of us; and the fair soul herself   125
Weigh'd between loathness and obedience at
Which end o' th' beam should bow. We have lost
   your son,
I fear, for ever. Milan and Naples have
Moe widows in them of this business' making,
Than we bring men to comfort them,   130
The fault's your own.

Alonso

             So is the dear'st o' th' loss.

134. *time* the right moment, suitable occasion.

136. *chirurgeonly* like a good surgeon.

137–8. *It is . . . cloudy* Gonzalo says that they are all depressed when the king is gloomy (overcast). The image of the king as the sun, here behind the clouds, and like them 'heavy' with weeping rain, is common in Shakespeare. In the metaphor there is perhaps an echo of the tempest weather.

138. *Fowl* a pun on *foul*? There may be a connection with *the old cock* (line 29).

139. *plantation* colonization. Gonzalo's meaning is deliberately misunderstood as 'planting' by Antonio.

140. *nettle-seed etc* i.e. weeds.

142. *want* lack. (Sebastian's remark anticipates 'king' Stephano's butt of wine in Act II, Scene ii; presumably he is thirsty and could do with a drink of wine at this moment.)

143–63. Gonzalo's description of an ideal society is probably derived from the writer Montaigne's essay on cannibals, published in English in 1603.

143–4. *I' th' commonwealth . . . things* in my ideal society I would see that everything was carried out in exactly the opposite manner to what is customary (i.e in normal states).

144–5. *no . . . admit* I wouldn't allow any trade of any kind.

144–5. *name of magistrate* title of magistrate (i.e. no one would be called 'magistrate').

146. *letters* learning, literacy.

147. *use of service* employing, and being employed as, servants.

147. *succession* inheritance.

148. *Bourn* boundary.

148. *tilth* tillage, ploughed land.

149. *No use . . . oil* i.e. because these are all examples of man's use of raw materials not being used by him in their raw state, *metal* comes from ore, *corn* has to be ground in a mill, *wine* pressed from grapes and *oil* from olives.

Gonzalo
    My lord Sebastian,
    The truth you speak doth lack some gentleness,
    And time to speak it in; you rub the sore,
    When you should bring the plaster.

Sebastian
                        Very well.   135

Antonio
    And most chirurgeonly.

Gonzalo
    It is foul weather in us all, good sir,
    When you are cloudy.

Sebastian
              Fowl weather?

Antonio
                        Very foul.

Gonzalo
    Had I plantation of this isle, my lord –

Antonio
    He'd sow 't with nettle-seed.

Sebastian
                   Or docks, or mallows.   140

Gonzalo
    And were the king on't, what would I do?

Sebastian
    Scape being drunk for want of wine.

Gonzalo
    I th' commonwealth I would by contraries
    Execute all things; for no kind of traffic
    Would I admit; no name of magistrate;   145
    Letters should not be known; riches, poverty,
    And use of service, none; contract, succession,
    Bourn, bound of land, tilth, vineyard, none;
    No use of metal, corn or wine, or oil;
    No occupation; all men idle, all;   150
    And women too, but innocent and pure;
    No sovereignty –

152–3. Sebastian and Antonio miss the point of Gonzalo's words by taking what he says too literally: Gonzalo is still trying to take Alonso's mind off the wreck. He may also be making deliberate mistakes in order to *minister occasion* (line 166) to *these gentlemen*.

155–6. *Treason, felony,/Sword* all three words are appropriate to the actions of Sebastian and Antonio later in the scene.
156. *engine* instrument or machine of war (or perhaps torture, e.g. the rack, if taken with *treason, felony,* for which crimes torture would be the punishment before execution; Montaigne says that it is worse 'to mangle by tortures and torments' a living body than to eat a dead one, in his essay on cannibals).
157. *bring forth* bear, produce.
157. *Of its own kind* of itself, without man's help.
158. *foison* plenty.
161. *all idle* Antonio scornfully repeats Gonzalo's words (line 148) and suggests that in the commonwealth of 'contraries', marriage (which requires hard work) will be replaced by purely sexual relationships between sluts and menservants.
163. *Save* God save.

167. *minister occasion* provide an opportunity.
168. *sensible* sensitive.
168. *use* are accustomed.

Sebastian
                Yet he would be king on't.

Antonio
  The latter end of his commonwealth forgets the
    beginning.

Gonzalo
  All things in common nature should produce
  Without sweat or endeavour. Treason, felony,   155
  Sword, pike, knife, gun, or need of any engine,
  Would I not have, but nature should bring forth,
  Of it own kind, all foison, all abundance,
  To feed my innocent people.

Sebastian
  No marrying 'mong his subjects?   160

Antonio
  None, man, all idle, whores and knaves.

Gonzalo
  I would with such perfection govern, sir,
  T' excel the golden age.

Sebastian
                Save his Majesty!

Antonio
  Long live Gonzalo!

Gonzalo
              And – do you mark me, sir?

Alonso
  Prithee, no more, thou dost talk nothing to me.   165

Gonzalo
  I do well believe your Highness; and did it to minister
  occasion to these gentlemen, who are of such sensible
  and nimble lungs that they always use to laugh at
  nothing.

Antonio
  'Twas you we laugh'd at.   170

Gonzalo
  Who in this kind of merry fooling am nothing to you;
  so you may continue, and laugh at nothing still.

174. *An* if.

174. *flat-long* with the flat of the blade (i.e it wasn't a cutting remark).

175. *brave mettle* fine spirit. Gonzalo uses *brave* ironically, and in *mettle* (metal) continues the image of a sword in *blow and flat-long*. After this verbal fencing, real swords will be drawn (line 287).

175–7. *you would . . . changing* in the Ptolemaic system of astronomy, still used in Shakespeare's time, the seven planets, of which the Moon was closest to the Earth, revolved in their spheres or orbits around the Earth, which was stationary at the centre of the whole system or 'World' (Universe). Gonzalo says that if the Moon remained unchanged, at the full, for more than a month, they (Sebastian and Antonio) would in their lunacy try to perform the impossible (i.e. lift it out of its natural course).

Stage Direction. *Ariel, invisible, playing* Where do you think Ariel stands as he plays his soothing music? Perhaps, as he is invisible, he shows his selection of those he wishes to put to sleep by standing by them as he plays, each in turn. The stately 'air' provides a change of key in the dialogue and introduces the sinister 'sleepy language' of the treacherous plotting.

178. *We would so, and then go a-bat-fowling* we would use the moon as a lantern (i.e. having taken it from its sphere) to attract roosting birds and then knock them down with sticks and clubs. Sebastian may also be referring to 'gulling' or tricking Gonzalo (with echoes, perhaps *of cock and fowl*).

179. *Nay . . . angry* perhaps this is in response to some gesture (hand on sword-hilt) of Gonzalo's, or possibly to provoke him further.

180–1. *No I. . . weakly* no, I assure you, I won't lose my temper over a triviality.

181–2. *Will you . . . heavy?* will you continue your feeble jokes until I yawn and fall asleep, for I am feeling very sleepy?

183. *Go sleep, and hear us* lie down, and listen to our laughter.

185. *with themselves* by closing their lids.

186. *inclin'd* being persuaded (by weariness pushing them in that direction).

187. *omit* ignore.

187. *heavy* sleepy.

191. *watch your safety* keep awake to guard your safety.

Antonio

What a blow was there given!

Sebastian

An it had not fall'n flat-long.

Gonzalo

You are gentlemen of brave mettle; you would lift   175
the moon out of her sphere, if she would continue in
it five weeks without changing.

[*Enter* ARIEL, *invisible, playing solemn music*]

Sebastian

We would so, and then go a-bat-fowling.

Antonio

Nay, good my lord, be not angry.

Gonzalo

No, I warrant you; I will not adventure my discretion 180
so weakly. Will you laugh me asleep, for I am very
heavy?

Antonio

Go sleep, and hear us.

[*All sleep but* ALONSO, SEBASTIAN *and* ANTONIO]

Alonso

What, all so soon asleep! I wish mine eyes
Would, with themselves, shut up my thoughts; I find 185
They are inclin'd to do so.

Sebastian

                              Please you, sir,
Do not omit the heavy offer of it:
It seldom visits sorrow; when it doth,
It is a comforter.

Antonio

                        We two, my lord,
Will guard your person while you take your rest,
And watch your safety.   190

Alonso

Thank you – wondrous heavy!

194. *quality* see Act I, Scene ii, line 337.

196. *my spirits are nimble* I'm wide awake, my mind is alert.

198. *thunder-stroke* as if struck by lightning.

201. *th' occasion speaks thee* the opportunity invites you (to make use of it).
202. *My strong imagination sees* my imagination is strongly convinced that it sees.
203. *waking* awake.

205. *sleepy language* i.e. words such as you might hear in a dream. (The repetition of 'sleep' and 's' alliterations gives the feelings of soft drowsiness.) The sleep-walking picture painted by Sebastian is strongly reminiscent in its language of *Macbeth* Act V, Scene i, lines 6–8.

210–11. *wink'st . . . waking* i.e. you are going around with your eyes shut (to your opportunities).

211. *distinctly* i.e. it is possible to distinguish a meaning in your snoring.

[ALONSO sleeps. Exit ARIEL]

Sebastian
What a strange drowsiness possesses them!
Antonio
It is the quality o' th' climate.
Sebastian
               Why
Doth it not then our eyelids sink? I find not   195
Myself dispos'd to sleep.
Antonio
               Nor I; my spirits are nimble.
They fell together all, as by consent;
They dropp'd, as by a thunder-stroke. What might,
Worthy Sebastian? O, what might! No more!
And yet methinks I see it in thy face,   200
What thou shouldst be, th' occasion speaks thee; and
My strong imagination sees a crown
Dropping upon thy head.
Sebastian
             What, art thou waking?

Antonio
Do you not hear me speak?
Sebastian
           I do; and surely
It is a sleepy language, and thou speak'st   205
Out of thy sleep. What is it thou didst say?
This is a strange repose, to be asleep
With eyes wide open; standing, speaking, moving,
And yet so fast asleep.
Antonio
           Noble Sebastian,
Thou let'st thy fortune sleep – die rather; wink'st   210
Whiles thou art waking.
Sebastian
           Thou dost snore distinctly;
There's meaning in thy snores.

213. *more serious than custom* Antonio says he is changing from his normal manner to get down to more serious business.

214. *if heed me* if you want to take in what I am going to say.

215. *Trebles thee o'er* makes you three times as great as you are now. (Perhaps Sebastian is three steps away from the throne – Alonso and his two children being in the way.)

215. *standing water* i.e. uncommitted, ready to be moved (like the sea, stationary for a time at high tide before it begins to ebb, or at low tide before it begins to rise).

216. *flow* rise (like the tide) in the world.

216–17. *to ebb . . . me* natural laziness persuades me to sink. As Alonso's younger brother, and not in line for the crown, Sebastian would naturally lack incentive to do more than drift.

218–20. *If you . . . invest it* if you could only see how much you welcome the idea (of removing Alonso) by pretending to reject the suggestion; how, in ridiculing the idea, you make it appear more attractive.

220. *invest* literally, clothe it.

220–2. *Ebbing . . . sloth* failures do indeed generally sink to the very bottom of society either through their lack of guts or sheer laziness. (The sea metaphor appears again in *standing water . . . ebb . . . ebbing . . . bottom.*)

223. *setting* fixed expression.

223–4. *proclaim . . . thee* tell me clearly what you have to say.

224–5. *a birth . . . yield* a subject which you find a good deal of difficulty in delivering (i.e. expressing).

226. *of weak remembrance* with a poor memory (perhaps a sign of old age?)

227. *as little memory* as little remembered (i.e. as soon forgotten as he himself forgets things).

228. *earth'd* buried. (Antonio is hinting towards the coming plot to kill Alonso and Gonzalo.)

229–30. *he's . . . persuade* Gonzalo is the model of persuasiveness, and his main occupation is diplomacy. (Antonio shows himself to be a subtle and powerful persuader of Sebastian in this scene, and is perhaps conscious of the irony in his description of Gonzalo.)

234–7. *No hope . . . there* having no hope in the possibility (that Ferdinand is alive) means that you have high hopes in another direction (the throne of Naples) and that even Ambition itself can do no more than see a short distance beyond (i.e. beyond the throne), but doubts finding anything worth aiming at there (because the throne of Naples is the highest target Ambition can aim at).

Antonio

    I am more serious than my custom; you
    Must be so too, if heed me; which to do
    Trebles thee o'er.

Sebastian

               Well, I am standing water.   215

Antonio

    I'll teach you how to flow.

Sebastian

             Do so: to ebb,
    Hereditary sloth instructs me.

Antonio

                    O,
    If you but knew how you the purpose cherish,
    Whiles thus you mock it! how, in stripping it,
    You more invest it! Ebbing men indeed,   220
    Most often, do so near the bottom run
    By their own fear or sloth.

Sebastian

               Prithee say on.
    The setting of thine eye and cheek proclaim
    A matter from thee, and a birth, indeed,
    Which throes thee much to yield.

Antonio

               Thus, sir: 225
    Although this lord of weak remembrance, this
    Who shall be of as little memory
    When he is earth'd, hath here almost persuaded –
    For he's a spirit of persuasion, only
    Professes to persuade – the King his son's alive,   230
    'Tis as impossible that he's undrown'd
    As he that sleeps here swims.

Sebastian

               I have no hope
    That he's undrown'd.

Antonio

             O, out of that 'no hope'
    What great hope have you! No hope that way is   235
    Another way so high a hope, that even

240–4. She . . . she . . . she . . . she the repetition becomes more and more sarcastic and the sentences longer as Antonio delivers his scornful exaggerations, designed to force Sebastian to act.

240. Queen of Tunis rhythmically balances *heir of Naples,* and by contrast places Claribel out of the running, i.e. she is *queen* and cannot be an *heir,* in *Tunis* and therefore cannot be in *Naples.*

241. Ten . . . life literally, thirty miles further than a journey which would take a man his whole life to accomplish.

242. no note no information, news.

242. post messenger.

244. from whom coming from whom.

245. cast vomited, thrown up (on to the shore). Ariel uses the same image at Act III, Scene iii, line 56. *Cast* then suggests actors in the following lines (246–8).

245–8. cast. . . discharge in *cast, perform, act, prologue,* and *discharge* there is a succession of theatrical terms. The *discharge,* in the sense of executing a performance (i.e. seeing that it is carried out), will be in 'producer' Prospero's hands and not Antonio's and Sebastian's, though.

249. stuff literally 'padding'. Sebastian, in his dry, cautious way, suggests that Antonio is being bombastic – speaking unnecessarily (bombast is cotton-wool used in padding clothes).

252. cubit approx. twenty inches, roughly a pace or step.

254. measure us retrace us (i.e. the cubits), return step by step.

255. wake arouse himself (from the *sleep* of lines 207–8).

256. seiz'd arrested, gripped.

258–9. prate . . . amply talk in as long-winded a way.

260–1. I . . . chat Antonio either means (a) that he could be as fond of speaking as Gonzalo or (b) that he could train *(make)* a jackdaw *(chough)* caw *(chat)* as profoundly *(deep)* i.e. Gonzalo's talk is as empty as a jackdaw's mimicking. (The alliteration of *chough* and *chat,* and the oxymoron in *deep chat* are good examples of Antonio's verbal energy.)

78

Ambition cannot pierce a wink beyond,
But doubt discovery there. Will you grant with me
That Ferdinand is drown'd?

Sebastian

He's gone.

Antonio

Then tell me,
Who's the next heir of Naples?

Sebastian

Claribel.

Antonio

She that is Queen of Tunis; she that dwells   240
Ten leagues beyond man's life; she that from Naples
Can have no note, unless the sun were post,
The Man i' th' Moon's too slow, till newborn chins
Be rough and razorable; she that from whom
We all were sea-swallow'd, though some cast again,   245
And by that destiny, to perform an act
Whereof what's past is prologue, what to come
In yours and my discharge.

Sebastian

What stuff is this! How say you?
'Tis true, my brother's daughter's Queen of Tunis;   250
So is she heir of Naples; 'twixt which regions
There is some space.

Antonio

A space whose ev'ry cubit
Seems to cry out 'How shall that Claribel
Measure us back to Naples? Keep in Tunis,
And let Sebastian wake'. Say this were death   255
That now hath seiz'd them; why, they were no worse
Than now they are. There be that can rule Naples
As well as he that sleeps; lords that can prate
As amply and unnecessarily
As this Gonzalo; I myself could make   260
A chough of as deep chat. O, that you bore
The mind that I do! What a sleep were this
For your advancement! Do you understand me?

264–5. *And how . . . fortune* and how does your desire *(content)* regard *(tender)* this lucky chance *(good fortune)*.

267. *And look . . . me* in Shakespeare robes often signify the ruler and disguise the rebel or plotter. (There is another reminder here of the drenching yet freshening effect of the sea.)

268. *feater* more neatly and gracefully (with the sense of being both worn with more confidence and being better tailored).

269. *fellows* see Act I, Scene ii, line 417 (note).

270. *But, for your conscience* but what about your conscience?

271–2. *If . . . slipper* if it were a blister on my heel, I'd have to wear a slipper. (The matter-of-fact reply shows how easily Antonio shrugs off any feeling of remorse.)

273. *This deity in my bosom* this god (conscience) ruling in my heart.

274–5. *candied . . . molest* may they (consciences) be no more than sugary sweets which dissolve before they prevent (me). The image is found elsewhere in Shakespeare and is associated with flattery, fawning dogs, 'sucking up', and sweets.

275. *brother* the repetition (lines 250, 266, 268) emphasizes the unnatural murder.

276–7. *No . . . dead* Alonso looks dead as he sleeps, and he would be no better than the earth he is lying on if he were dead. (Antonio's suggestion that Alonso might as well be dead is an attempt to stop Sebastian thinking too deeply about the the situation.)

278. *obedient . . . of it* only three inches of Antonio's trusty servant, his sword, are required to reach Alonso's heart. (Perhaps Antonio draws his sword a few inches from its scabbard and thrusts it back again at *lay to bed.)*

280. *wink* sleep 'shut-eye' *(perpetual wink:* death). The combination *of perpetual* and *for aye* (for ever) reinforces the finality of the action ('for ever and ever, amen').

281. *morsel* scrap (of food, flesh). Shakespeare often associates 'morsel' with death (which consumes the flesh, body).

281. *Sir Prudence* mocking the cautious Gonzalo, and possibly a reminder of line 42. If so, Gonzalo *(Sir)* is an 'old maid' *(Prudence)* rather than a gallant knight (e.g. Sir Lancelot).

282. *upbraid* criticize, condemn.

282–5. *For . . . hour* i.e. the other courtiers, as ready to be tempted as a cat is to lap up milk, will agree to any explanation by him and Sebastian.

285–6. *case . . . precedent* Sebastian uses legal terms *(case . . . precedent)* to justify, perhaps with a sense of irony, their intended crime: i.e. 'because you have established a precedent (recognized way of proceeding) I can now follow your line of behaviour on what I shall do.'

Sebastian
    Methinks I do.
Antonio
               And how does your content
    Tender your own good fortune?
Sebastian
                   I remember   265
    You did supplant your brother Prospero.
Antonio
                       True.
    And look how well my garments sit upon me,
    Much feater than before. My brother's servants
    Were then my fellows; now they are my men.
Sebastian
    But, for your conscience –   270
Antonio
    Ay, sir, where lies that? If 'twere a kibe,
    'Twould put me to my slipper, but I feel not
    This deity in my bosom; twenty consciences
    That stand 'twixt me and Milan, candied be they
    And melt, ere they molest! Here lies your brother,   275
    No better than the earth he lies upon,
    If he were that which now he's like – that's dead;
    Whom I with this obedient steel, three inches of it,
    Can lay to bed for ever; whiles you, doing thus,
    To the perpetual wink for aye might put   280
    This ancient morsel, this Sir Prudence, who
    Should not upbraid our course. For all the rest,
    They'll take suggestion as a cat laps milk;
    They'll tell the clock to any business that
    We say befits the hour.
Sebastian
                 Thy case, dear friend,   285
    Shall be my precedent; as thou got'st Milan,
    I'll come by Naples. Draw thy sword. One stroke
    Shall free thee from the tribute which thou payest;
    And I the King shall love thee.
Antonio

289. *Draw together* let's unsheathe our swords at the same time.

291. *Gonzalo* Antonio is not asking Sebastian to kill his brother; he (Antonio) will kill Alonso, while Sebastian kills Gonzalo. (Furthermore, Antonio will be quite sure if he kills Alonso personally of being free from the tribute he pays to him.)

291. *O, but one word* this is perhaps a rather obvious dramatic device to allow Ariel time to rouse Gonzalo, and, if they withdraw to the rear of the stage, or to one side, space for him to move in.

293. *his friend* i.e. Gonzalo (see Act I, Scene ii, lines 161–2). Ariel is here speaking to the audience, addressing Gonzalo impersonally and telling the audience that he has come to keep *them* (Alonso and Gonzalo) alive.

294. *project dies* plan is ruined, purpose fails.

295. *snoring* i.e. in exhausted sleep.

296. *open-ey'd conspiracy* traitors who are awake.

297. *His time doth take* seizes his opportunity.

301. *sudden* swift, speedy.

302. *Preserve the King!* loyal Gonzalo's first thought is for his master's safety.

305. *ghastly looking* Antonio and Sebastian are pale and grim-faced (like ghosts), presumably with a combination of horror and determination at the thought of committing a cold-blooded murder, but may also be shocked at being discovered with swords drawn. Is Alonso suspicious?

306–9. It is interesting that it is Sebastian rather than the previously more voluble Antonio who speaks first, perhaps he is the 'cooler customer' of the two. On the other hand, it may simply be that he is standing over Gonzalo, about to kill him, and therefore replies to him.

307. *hollow* echoing, reverberating. *Hollow* can also mean false, which is what the fictitious *bellowing* was.

           Draw together;

And when I rear my hand, do you the like,   290
To fall it on Gonzalo.

Sebastian

          O, but one word.

[They talk apart]

[Re-enter ARIEL, *invisible, with music and song]*

Ariel

My master through his art foresees the danger
That you, his friend, are in; and sends me forth –
For else his project dies – to keep them living.

[Sings in GONZALO'S *ear]*

While you here do snoring lie,   295
    Open-ey'd conspiracy
His time doth take.
If of life you keep a care,
Shake off slumber, and beware.
    Awake, awake!   300

Antonio

Then let us both be sudden.

Gonzalo

          Now, good angels

Preserve the King!

[They wake]

Alonso

Why, how now? – Ho, awake! –
Why are you drawn?
Wherefore this ghastly looking?

Gonzalo

          What's the matter?   305

Sebastian

Whiles we stood here securing your repose,
Even now, we heard a hollow burst of bellowing
Like bulls, or rather lions, did't not wake you?

310. *din* although Sebastian and Antonio are inventing noises of wild beasts to explain away their drawn swords, travellers' tales of the period mention terrifying sounds being heard on unexplored islands. It is ironical that Prospero's island is in fact *full of noises,* as Caliban says (Act III, Scene ii, line 131).

310. *monster's* a monster is an unnatural creature, but not necessarily a large one (i.e Caliban is viewed as a monster, but is no larger than a human). It is ironical that Antonio (who perhaps replies to Alonso because he is standing over *him)* is himself a 'monster' of a different sort – i.e a potential murderer.

313. *humming* i.e. Ariel's song (compare Act III, Scene ii, line 134).

315. *cried* cried out.

320. *Heavens . . . beasts* Gonzalo may suspect Sebastian and Antonio, in which case *beasts* could refer to them; even if he does not, the audience would be aware of the irony.

By the end of this scene we have begun to sympathize a little with Alonso, because of his 'dead' son and the plot on his life: he is ripe for repentance and forgiveness. Antonio and Sebastian, in contrast, have increased in guilt. All *three men of sin,* when they next appear (in Act III, scene iii), reach the turning point of their part of the play's action when they are forced to recognise their guilt.

It struck mine ear most terribly.

Alonso

I heard nothing.

Antonio

O, 'twas a din to fright a monster's ear,   310
To make an earthquake! Sure it was the roar
Of a whole herd of lions.

Alonso

Heard you this, Gonzalo?

Gonzalo

Upon mine honour, sir, I heard a humming,
And that a strange one too, which did awake me;
I shak'd you, sir, and cried; as mine eyes open'd,   315
I saw their weapons drawn – there was a noise,
That's verily. 'Tis best we stand upon our guard,
Or that we quit this place. Let's draw our weapons.

Alonso

Lead off this ground, and let's make further search
For my poor son.

Gonzalo

Heavens keep him from these beasts! 320
For he is, sure, i' th' island.

Alonso

Lead away.

Ariel

Prospero my lord shall know what I have done;
So, King, go safely on to seek thy son.

[Exeunt]

SCENE II

The third situation is now developed when Caliban meets Trinculo, the royal jester, and Stephano, the royal butler. They form a comic parallel to the *three men of sin* (Alonso, Sebastian and Antonio), and like them also plot to take power. However, their clowning gives the audience an opportunity to relax and laugh, though as always in Shakespeare's plays the comedy is used to mirror the main action and deepen its meaning.

Stage Direction, **burden of wood** the opening of this scene is identical with that of Act III, Scene i, with the parallel, log-bearing situation underlining the contrast between Caliban and Ferdinand.

2. *flats* swamps. (The force of the words *fens, flats, fall* is considerable; as Caliban has said, his profit from learning language is that he knows how to curse.)

3. *inch-meal* inch by inch, measured in inches *(meal:* measure).

5. *urchin-shows* hobgoblin apparitions.

5. *pitch* throw, toss (with perhaps a play on *pitch* tar, i.e. he will be dirtied by being pitched into the mud).

6. *firebrand* flaming torch.

9. *mow* make a mocking expression.

11. *tumbling* rolling.

11. *mount* raise.

12. *pricks* prickles, spikes.

13. *wound* entwined with.

Stage Direction. **Trinculo** dressed probably in a jester's costume, wet, shivering, and scared of being the only survivor. Caliban mistakes him for one of Prospero's spirits because of his strange appearance.

15. *and to* in order to.

17. *mind* notice.

18. *bear off* keep off, ward off.

19. *weather* storm, tempest.

19. *brewing* being prepared (suggesting *liquor* in line 21, which in turn anticipates Stephano's bottle of sack).

21. *foul bombard* (a) a large leathern jug, (b) a siege cannon. Both meanings are present here: the black cloud is about to empty its contents, and the thunder cloud to roar out (compare descriptions of the tempest in Act I). It is *foul* because it is discharging 'dirty weather'.

21–2. *shed his liquor* i.e. the black cloud will empty its contents (rain). There may also be a suggestion either of vomiting or urinating; Trinculo's humour is repeatedly quite crude (compare *backward voice,* line 93, *siege,* line 107, and *vent,* line 107).

27. *a kind of . . . Poor-John* a sort of not at all fresh dried hake (i.e. with a very unpleasant smell).

Scene II

Another part of the island.

[Enter CALIBAN*, with a burden of wood.*
A noise of thunder heard]

Caliban

All the infections that the sun sucks up
From bogs, fens, flats, on Prosper fall, and make him
By inch-meal a disease! His spirits hear me,
And yet I needs must curse. But they'll nor pinch,
Fright me with urchin-shows, pitch me i' th' mire,   5
Nor lead me, like a firebrand, in the dark
Out of my way, unless he bid 'em; but
For every trifle are they set upon me;
Sometime like apes that mow and chatter at me,
And after bite me; then like hedgehogs which   10
Lie tumbling in my barefoot way, and mount
Their pricks at my footfall; sometime am I
All wound with adders, who with cloven tongues
Do hiss me into madness.

[Enter TRINCULO*]*

Lo, now, lo!
Here comes a spirit of his, and to torment me   15
For bringing wood in slowly. I'll fall flat,
Perchance he will not mind me.

Trinculo

Here's neither bush nor shrub to bear off any weather
at all, and another storm brewing, I hear it sing i' th'
wind. Yond same black cloud, yond huge one, looks   20
like a foul bombard that would shed his liquor. If it
should thunder as it did before, I know not where to
hide my head. Yond same cloud cannot choose but
fall by pailfuls. What have we here? a man or a fish?   25
dead or alive? A fish: he smells like a fish; a very ancient
and fish-like smell, a kind of not-of-the-newest

27–8. *A strange fish!* an odd creature! Caliban may smell like a fish. Having just survived drowning, Trinculo may have his mind filled with fish; probably he simply means something is 'fishy', meaning 'suspicious'.

29. *painted* i.e. a painted sign at a fair to attract the curious to 'walk up' and see the 'strange fish', a novelty from a distant land.

30. *piece of silver* i.e. more than just a copper coin.

31. *monster make a man* (a) make a man's fortune, (b) be taken for a man (pass as one).

32. *give a doit* give a farthing, give a sou. (A doit was a small Dutch coin of low value.)

33. *lay out* spend.

34. *Indian* an inhabitant of the New World (America). Many were brought to Europe in Shakespeare's time to be displayed as curiosities, but few survived their contact with 'civilization'. (Trinculo suggests in line 27 that he would make a great profit from Caliban in England.)

34. *his fins like arms* This does not mean that Caliban's arms look like fins, but simply that Trinculo, expecting to find fins on his fish, is surprised to find arms instead.

35. *Warm* i.e. unlike a cold-blooded fish.

39. *gaberdine* cloak.

40–41. *Misery . . . bedfellow* a proverbial saying meaning 'when you are down on your luck, you may have to lay your head anywhere'.

41. *shroud* shelter, take cover.

41. *dregs* i.e. the last drops.

Stage Direction. *Enter Stephano:* his smutty and tipsy songs contrast with Ariel's delicate airs.

45. *scurvy* fever contracted by sailors due to lack of the right vitamins, here meaning simply – 'rotten'.

45–6. *at a man's funeral* i.e. his own, just referred to in *die ashore,* or possibly Trinculo's, presumed drowned. Stephano is depressed in his drunkenness.

47. *swabber* scrubber of the decks. The irony of Stephano's including himself in the list of genuine sailors, *master, boatswain,* etc., is that he is *not* a sailor and is on his first voyage.

49. *Mall* Maud.

49. *Meg* Margaret.

51. *tang* sting (i.e. a sharp tongue).

53. *She . . . pitch* i.e. she didn't like the smell of a ship, or of those from a ship.

54. *Yet . . . itch* i.e. might be intimate with her. (*Tailor, scratch,* and *itch* probably all have sexual connotations.)

Poor-John. A strange fish! Were I in England now, as
once I was, and had but this fish painted, not a holiday
fool there but would give a piece of silver. There would   30
this monster make a man; any strange beast there
makes a man; when they will not give a doit to relieve
a lame beggar, they will lay out ten to see a dead
Indian. Legg'd like a man, and his fins like arms! Warm,
o' my troth! I do now let loose my opinion; hold it   35
no longer: this is no fish, but an islander, that hath
lately suffered by a thunderbolt.
[Thunder] Alas, the storm is come again! My best way
is to creep under his gaberdine; there is no other shelter
hereabout. Misery acquaints a man with strange   40
bedfellows. I will here shroud till the dregs of the storm
be past.

[Enter STEPHANO *singing, a bottle in his hand]*

Stephano
    I shall no more to sea, to sea,
    Here shall I die ashore –
    This is a very scurvy tune to sing at a man's   45
    funeral, well, here's my comfort.

[Drinks]

    The master, the swabber, the boatswain, and I,
    The gunner, and his mate,
    Lov'd Mall, Meg, and Marian, and Margery,
    But none of us car'd for Kate,   50
    For she had a tongue with a tang,
    Would cry to a sailor 'Go hang!'
    She lov'd not the savour of tar nor of pitch,
    Yet a tailor might scratch her where'er she did itch.
    Then to sea, boys, and let her go hang!   55

This is a scurvy tune too; but here's my comfort.

[Drinks]

57. *Do not torment me* Trinculo, trembling with fear that Stephano's voice (which he presumably recognizes) is that of a ghost (see line 86), is thought by Caliban to be a spirit preparing to torment him.

58. *What's the matter?* what's this?

58–9. *Do you ... of Ind?* are you (devils, spirits) trying to deceive me by appearing as savages and Indians?

61. *four legs* Caliban's two legs point from under his gaberdine in one direction and Trinculo's in the other.

61–3. *As proper ... ground* as excellent a man as ever walked on four legs (Stephano changes the proverbial 'two' to 'four' to match the Caliban–Trinculo monster he is looking at) cannot make this fellow (i.e. Caliban–Trinculo) retreat.

67. *ague* fever (because both Caliban and Trinculo are shaking with fear).

68. *should he learn* could he have learnt.

69. *recover* revive. (Stephano's immediate reaction to this 'islander' is to help him, but only so that he can then exploit him. This attitude resembles how many of the explorers and colonists of the time felt.)

70–1. *a present for* a suitable present for.

71–2. *neat's leather* cowhide (shoes).

75. *fit* mad spasm.

75–6. *after the wisest* very sensibly.

78–9. *I will ... for him* i.e. I shall expect a high price for him.

Caliban

Do not torment me. O!

Stephano

What's the matter? Have we devils here? Do you put
tricks upon 's with savages and men of Ind? Ha! I have
not scap'd drowning to be afeard now of your four   60
legs; for it hath been said: As proper a man as ever
went on four legs cannot make him give ground; and
it shall be said so again, while Stephano breathes at
nostrils.

Caliban

The spirit torments me. O!   65

Stephano

This is some monster of the isle with four legs, who
hath got, as I take it, an ague. Where the devil
should he learn our language? I will give him some
relief, if it be but for that. If I can recover him, and
keep him tame, and get to Naples with him, he's a   70
present for any emperor that ever trod on neat's
leather.

Caliban

Do not torment me, prithee, I'll bring my wood home
faster.

Stephano

He's in his fit now, and does not talk after the wisest.   75
He shall taste of my bottle; if he have never drunk
wine afore, it will go near to remove his fit. If I can
recover him, and keep him tame, I will not take too
much for him; he shall pay for him that hath him,
and that soundly.   80

Caliban

Thou dost me yet but little hurt; thou wilt anon, I
know it by thy trembling; now Prosper works upon
thee.

85. *language to you, cat* proverbially, liquor could make a cat speak. Prospero has already given Caliban language, and all that liquor is going to do is to make him a *howling monster* (line 177). By *give language* Stephano means 'loosen your tongue'. (The number of proverbs spoken in this scene may indicate the lower-class characters, who rely on proverbs to face life's hardships. The use of repetitive phrases by Stephano may be a further indication of his limited intelligence and level in society, e.g. *scurvy tune, if I can recover him, and keep him tame, and that soundly, open your mouth.*)

87. *you . . . friend* you seem unable to understand that I'm your friend.

88. *chaps* jaws.

90. *O, defend me!* Trinculo invokes the aid of good angels to keep off devils.

91. *delicate* cleverly constructed.

92–3. *forward . . . backward* his voice in front pays compliments and his voice behind is rude and insulting. (There seem to be two ideas at work in what Stephano is saying: (a) he is calling the monster literally and metaphorically 'two-faced', (b) he is echoing Trinculo's *let loose*, line 35, in *backward voice . . . foul*, which in turn prepares for the reference to *vent*, line 107.)

95. *Come – Amen!* come on, drink up whoa! that's enough!

100. *I . . . spoon* another proverb, i.e. that anyone supping with the Devil has need of a long spoon.

101–2. *Stephano . . . Trinculo* Shakespeare fixes their names in the audience's minds by repetition: each name is used six times in this short dialogue.

101. *touch me* i.e. to show that he is Stephano and not a spirit. (Compare Prospero's embracing Alonso, Act V, Scene i, lines 108–9.)

102. *be not afeard* i.e. that I am a devil.

105. *Trinculo's legs* perhaps recognizable because of the jester's leggings, or because they are *lesser*, thinner than Caliban's muscular and possibly misshapen legs.

106. *very* truly.

107. *siege* excrement. *Siege* primarily meant 'seat', and 'stool' is still used to refer to faeces. Trinculo has appeared from Caliban's 'behind'.

107. *moon-calf* i.e. the Moon's astrological influence has caused Caliban to be deformed before birth and has produced a misshapen monster.

107. *vent* let out.

109–10. *I hope . . . drown'd* i.e. that he (Trinculo) is not talking to the ghost of a drowned Stephano.

113. *two Neopolitans scap'd* another use of dramatic irony (in that the audience knows of other citizens of Naples who have escaped drowning).

Stephano

Come on your ways; open your mouth; here is that
which will give language to you, cat. Open your mouth; 85
this will shake your shaking, I can tell you, and that
soundly; you cannot tell who's your friend. Open your
chaps again.

Trinculo

I should know that voice; it should be – but he is
drown'd; and these are devils. O, defend me! 90

Stephano

Four legs and two voices; a most delicate monster! His
forward voice, now, is to speak well of his friend;
his backward voice is to utter foul speeches and to
detract. If all the wine in my bottle will recover him,
I will help his ague. Come – Amen! I will pour some 95
in thy other mouth.

Trinculo

Stephano!

Stephano

Doth thy other mouth call me?
Mercy, mercy! This is a devil, and no monster;
I will leave him, I have no long spoon. 100

Trinculo

Stephano! If thou beest Stephano, touch me, and speak
to me; for I am Trinculo – be not afeard – thy good
friend Trinculo.

Stephano

If thou beest Trinculo, come forth; I'll pull thee by the
lesser legs; if any be Trinculo's legs, these are they. 105
Thou art very Trinculo indeed! How cam'st thou to be
the siege of this moon-calf? Can he vent Trinculos?

Trinculo

I took him to be kill'd with a thunderstroke. But art
thou not drown'd, Stephano? I hope now thou are not
drown'd. Is the storm overblown? I hid me under the 110
dead moon-calf's gaberdine for fear of the storm. And
art thou living, Stephano? O Stephano, two Neapolitans
scap'd!

114. *turn me about* i.e. perhaps Trinculo in his excitement is dancing round and round with him.

115. *constant* settled.

116. *These . . . sprites* 'these are certainly fine beings if they are not spirits.' (Perhaps Caliban suspects that they must be spirits, to be so fine.)

120. *Swear by this bottle* i.e. Stephano is blasphemously using the bottle as a Bible (compare *kiss the book,* i.e. the bottle, in line 125).

122. *heaved overboard* either to lighten the ship in case it was running into shallow water or as something buoyant to cling to (as Stephano does) when they abandon ship.

131. *like a goose* the meaning is unclear. Possibly (a) he is (being a Jester or Court Fool) a 'giddy goose', or mad, (b) long-necked like the goose rather than short-necked like the duck, a reference to his taking a long drink from the bottle, (c) lecherous ('goose' being associated with venereal disease in some of Shakespeare's plays).

137. *Out o' th' moon* Stephano, as many travellers were doing at that time, uses the native's innocent belief in what he is told: he is delighted that Caliban should think him a god.

138. *when time was* once upon a time.

Stephano

Prithee, do not turn me about; my stomach is not
constant.   115

Caliban

[Aside] These be fine things, an if they be not sprites.
That's a brave god, and bears celestial liquor.
I will kneel to him.

Stephano

How didst thou scape? How cam'st thou hither? Swear
by this bottle how thou cam'st hither – I escap'd   120
upon a butt of sack, which the sailors heaved
o'erboard – by this bottle, which I made of the bark
of a tree, with mine own hands, since I was cast
ashore.

Caliban

I'll swear upon that bottle to be thy true subject, for   125
the liquor is not earthly.

Stephano

Here; swear then how thou escap'dst.

Trinculo

Swum ashore, man, like a duck, I can swim like a duck,
I'll be sworn.

Stephano

[Passing the bottle] Here, kiss the book. Though thou   130
canst swim like a duck, thou art made like a goose.

Trinculo

O Stephano, hast any more of this?

Stephano

The whole butt, man; my cellar is in a rock by th'
seaside, where my wine is hid. How now, mooncalf!
How does thine ague?   135

Caliban

Hast thou not dropp'd from heaven?

Stephano

Out o' th' moon, I do assure thee; I was the Man i'
th' Moon, when time was.

139. *adore thee* worship you (perhaps suitably, as a *mooncalf*).

140. *thee . . . bush* the patterns on the moon's surface portrayed the Man, who, with his dog, had been exiled to the Moon (according to popular legend) for gathering brushwood on a Sunday. His *bush* was his bundle of brushwood.

141–2. *furnish . . . contents* i.e. fill it up again soon with more wine.

143. *By . . . light* upon my soul.

143. *shallow* ignorant, credulous.

144. *weak* foolish.

145. *Well drawn* that was a good swig.

147. *every . . . inch* Caliban possesses local knowledge of the island, and unless he shows the new settlers (which is what Stephano and Trinculo represent) the fertile parts they will soon starve.

149–50. *perfidious . . . asleep* (a) the treacherous behaviour of initially friendly natives was often reported by colonists in the New World, (b) in Act III, Scene ii, line 58, Caliban proposes to kill Prospero in his sleep.

153. *puppy-headed* stupid.

155–7. *beat him . . . in drink* the cowardly Trinculo, resenting Caliban's doglike devotion to Stephano, says that he would like to beat the kneeling Caliban. Perhaps Caliban turns on him and is only prevented from attacking him by Stephano's sudden *Come, kiss*. Trinculo then saves his face by saying that he would not take unfair advantage of Caliban anyway, i.e. beat him when he's drunk.

159–63. *thee* the repetition of *thee* in these lines shows Caliban transferring his allegiance from Prospero *(the tyrant)* to Stephano *(wondrous man)*, but may also underline his dislike of Trinculo, which is used by Ariel (in Act III, Scene ii, lines 40–80).

163. *wondrous man* Caliban's admiration of Stephano can be contrasted with Ferdinand's of Miranda (Act I, Scene ii, line 427).

Caliban

I have seen thee in her, and I do adore thee. My
mistress show'd me thee, and thy dog and thy bush. 140

Stephano

Come, swear to that; kiss the book. I will furnish it
anon with new contents. Swear.

[CALIBAN drinks]

Trinculo

By this good light, this is a very shallow monster! I
afeard of him! A very weak monster! The Man i' th'
Moon! A most poor credulous monster! Well drawn, 145
monster, in good sooth!

Caliban

I'll show thee every fertile inch o' th' island; and I
will kiss thy foot. I prithee be my god.

Trinculo

By this light, a most perfidious and drunken
monster! When 's god's asleep he'll rob his bottle. 150

Caliban

I'll kiss thy foot, I'll swear myself thy subject.

Stephano

Come on, then, down, and swear.

Trinculo

I shall laugh myself to death at this puppy-headed
monster. A most scurvy monster! I could find in my
heart to beat him – 155

Stephano

Come, kiss.

Trinculo

But that the poor monster's in drink. An
abominable monster!

Caliban

I'll show thee the best springs, I'll pluck thee berries,
I'll fish for thee, and get thee wood enough. 160
A plague upon the tyrant that I serve!
I'll bear him no more sticks, but follow thee,
Thou wondrous man.

166. *crabs* crab-apples.

167. *pig-nuts* earth-nuts.

169. *marmoset* small edible monkey.

170. *filberts* hazelnuts.

171. *scamels* the meaning is uncertain, but possible means 'god-wit', a curlew-like marsh bird; also possibly a 'sea-mell' or seamew.

174. *we will inherit* I, as king, will take possession (as next in line after Alonso, Ferdinand etc whom he believes are all dead).

174. *bear my bottle* i.e. as royal cupbearer. Caliban's worship of Stephano, and Stephano's drunkenness, make the royal butler behave condescendingly towards his equal, or near-equal, the royal jester, who now has the menial task of carrying the royal cup.

175. *Fellow Trinculo* to address a servant as 'fellow' if you were his superior was acceptable, but to address an equal as 'fellow' was a gross insult. Stephano is drunk with power as well as wine.

178. *No more . . . fish* natives of the New World used to help the early colonists by building dams so that fish could be got more easily, thus providing food without which they would often have starved.

179. *firing* firewood.

180. *At requiring* on demand.

181. *trenchering* wooden plates cleaned of food by *scraping*.

182. *Ca – Caliban* possibly a drunken 'hiccup'.

184. *Freedom* Caliban is in fact even less free than before, the servant of a servant, and slave to a bottle.

184. *high-day!* Holiday (perhaps granted to celebrate the accession of King Stephano?).

186. *Lead the way* The tipsy trio make a procession, Caliban leading, and Trinculo following Stephano. There is an ironic comment in this upon the end of the previous scene, when Alonso says *lead away* and the royal party proceeds on its way in search of Ferdinand.

By the end of Act II the initial development of each of the three situations is complete and the key characters of the play have displayed their personalities in response to them. Each group is being (or, in the case of Ferdinand and Miranda, has already been) drawn towards Prospero's cell, partly by Ariel's music and partly by their own motivation.

Trinculo

    A most ridiculous monster, to make a wonder of a
    poor drunkard!   165

Caliban

    I prithee let me bring thee where crabs grow;
    And I with my long nails will dig thee pig-nuts;
    Show thee a jay's nest, and instruct thee how
    To snare the nimble marmoset; I'll bring thee
    To clust'ring filberts, and sometimes I'll get thee   170
    Young scamels from the rock. Wilt thou go with me?

Stephano

    I prithee now, lead the way without any more talking.
    Trinculo, the King and all our company else being
    drown'd, we will inherit here. Here, bear my bottle.
    Fellow Trinculo, we'll fill him by and by again.   175

Caliban

    [Sings drunkenly] Farewell, master; farewell, farewell!

Trinculo

    A howling monster, a drunken monster!

Caliban

        No more dams I'll make for fish,
        Nor fetch in firing
        At requiring,   180
        Nor scrape trenchering, nor wash dish.
        'Ban 'Ban, Ca – Caliban,
        Has a new master – Get a new man.

    Freedom, high-day! high-day, freedom! freedom
    high-day, freedom!   185

Stephano

    O brave monster! Lead the way.

                  [Exeunt]

ACT III, SCENE I

This scene stands at the mid-point of the play and provides its turning-point, when Ferdinand and Miranda declare their love for one another; from this point there is no going back, Prospero's plans can now proceed too, and this declaration of love between the two young people makes possible the healing of the wounds of the older generation.

Stage Direction, ***bearing a log*** the contrast between Ferdinand and Caliban (who has just said in his song that he will not *fetch in firing At requiring*) is made clear. Perhaps the log is large enough to be used as a seat for Ferdinand's opening speech.

1–2. *There . . . sets off* some forms of recreation can be quite tough, and the pleasure they provide makes up for the effort they demand.

2. *baseness* servant's work.

3. *nobly undergone* accepted because they lead (i.e. the menial tasks) to noble results.

4. *mean task* basic, unpleasant job.

5. *odious* hateful.

5. *but* except for the fact that.

6. *mistress . . . serve* Ferdinand uses the words of a gallant medieval knight. It is his duty to perform her every wish without complaint.

6. *quickens* revives me (literally 'raises me from the dead').

8. *crabbed* sour, hard, 'difficult' (in contrast to the *gentle* Miranda, sweet, kind, and compassionate).

11. *Upon a sore injunction* under threat of severe punishment.

11–12. *sweet . . . Weeps . . . sees* the very sound of Miranda's voice is in these alliterations and assonances.

12–13. *such . . . executor* such a dull job never had anyone as noble to perform it.

13.1 *forget* i.e. I must get on with the job. Rested, he probably stands up to resume his labours.

15. *Most . . . do it* i.e. I am most busily engaged (in thinking of Miranda) when I am least busily engaged (in doing my job).

Stage Direction, ***at a distance*** perhaps just outside his cell. On the raised rear level of the stage at an indoor performance, the position of the godlike father-figure of Prospero would be impressive, involved yet detached; particularly so when he calls on the heavens to bless the couple (lines 75–6).

17. *enjoin'd* obliged by oath.

18–19. *when . . . weep* when this log is burning it will ooze with resin (i.e. nature will sympathize with you, as I do, by weeping). Compare Act I, Scene ii, line 150, where the winds are described as sighing in sympathy.

ACT THREE

Scene I

Before Prospero's cell.

[Enter FERDINAND, bearing a log]

Ferdinand

There be some sports are painful, and their labour
Delight in them sets off; some kinds of baseness.
Are nobly undergone, and most poor matters
Point to rich ends. This my mean task
Would be as heavy to me as odious, but   5
The mistress which I serve quickens what's dead,
And makes my labours pleasures. O, she is
Ten times more gentle than her father's crabbed,
And he's compos'd of harshness. I must remove
Some thousands of these logs, and pile them up,   10
Upon a sore injunction; my sweet mistress
Weeps when she sees me work, and says such
    baseness
Had never like executor. I forget;
But these sweet thoughts do even refresh my
    labours,
Most busy, least when I do it.

[Enter MIRANDA; and PROSPERO at a distance, unseen]

Miranda

                              Alas, now; pray you,   15
Work not so hard; I would the lightning had
Burnt up those logs that you are enjoin'd to pile.
Pray, set it down and rest you; when this burns,
'Twill weep for having wearied you. My father
Is hard at study, pray, now, rest yourself,   20

21. *safe* safely out of the way. Another obvious dramatic irony, as Prospero is standing *unseen* behind them.

22. *The sun . . . set* together with Miranda's *these three hours,* this is a reminder of time passing, and perhaps suggests the folk-tale situation of a young suitor given an almost impossible task to complete (as a test of his manhood) before sundown in order to win a fair princess.

24. *the while* for the time being. Rhyming seems to occur in *while . . . pile, crack . . . back, do it. . . to if,* and the formality and artificiality given by rhyme are supported by the balanced alternation of identically-organized short speeches from Ferdinand and Miranda, i.e. *O most dear . . . strive to do* is mirrored by *If you'll. . . the pile,* and *No, precious . . . sit lazy by* by *It would . . . it is against.* These sound almost like an operatic duet between a perfectly-paired set of lovers.

26. *crack* strain (pull a muscle).

28. *become me* be as fitting for me.

30. *much more ease* much more readily.

31-2. *Poor . . . shows it* poor creature, you are strongly affected by love! This 'attack' shows that clearly. (Miranda is described as having caught the 'plague' of love.)

33-4. *'tis . . . night* Ferdinand doesn't mean this literally (they have only known each other for an hour or two of daylight), i.e. she revives him as dawn does by being with him during his 'dead' time (night) of log-lugging.

35. *in my prayers* i.e. a suitable setting for the name *of goddess,* perhaps like a rich jewel.

37. *broke your hest* disobeyed your command.

37. *Admir'd Miranda* the name Miranda means 'worthy to be wondered at' or 'worthy of admiration'.

39. *What's . . . world* e.g. the richest or most precious object.

40. *ey'd with best regard* been attracted to by their looks.

41-2. *Th' harmony . . . ear* my ear has been captivated by the sweet music of their voices. The senses of sight and hearing, so often referred to in the play, are again present in lines 40-2.

42. *several* separate, different.

He's safe for these three hours.
Ferdinand
                      O most dear mistress,
The sun will set before I shall discharge
What I must strive to do.
Miranda
                     If you'll sit down,
I'll bear your logs the while, pray give me that,
I'll carry it to the pile.
Ferdinand
                  No, precious creature,   25
I had rather crack my sinews, break my back,
Than you should such dishonour undergo,
While I sit lazy by.
Miranda
                  It would become me
As well as it does you; and I should do it
With much more ease, for my good will is to it,   30
And yours it is against.
Prospero
[Aside]   Poor worm, thou art infected!
This visitation shows it.
Miranda
                You look wearily.
Ferdinand
No, noble mistress; 'tis fresh morning with me
When you are by at night. I do beseech you,
Chiefly that I might set it in my prayers,   35
What is your name?
Miranda
             Miranda – O my father,
I have broke your hest to say so!
Ferdinand
               Admir'd Miranda!
Indeed the top of admiration; worth
What's dearest to the world! Full many a lady
I have ey'd with best regard; and many a time   40
Th' harmony of their tongues hath into bondage
Brought my too diligent ear; for several virtues

43–5. never . . . ow'd never any one of them, for, however perfect, she always had some failing.

46. put it to the foil the *defect* cancelled out the *grace*

47. peerless unrivalled.

48. every creature's best the best quality of every being.

37–48. Ferdinand's speech contains a considerable number of repetitions (*Admir'd* and *Miranda, many . . . many, several. . . several, you, O you, created . . . creature*) which perhaps add to the lyrical and song-like effect. It is as if Ferdinand is rejoicing at the gift of Miranda's name.

50. glass mirror.

52. features appearance (not simply faces), what people look like.

52. abroad in the world generally.

53. I am skilless of I have no idea.

54. jewel in my dower Miranda has nothing (which is, in fact, everything) to offer this prince (now, apparently, a king) in the way of dowry to give him when they are married but the most precious quality she can possess, her 'modesty'. (The jewel image is repeated.)

56–7. Nor . . . like of nor can my imagination create any being other than you whom I would want.

58. precepts instructions, (presumably not to talk too much to Ferdinand, which might seem 'forward' or immodest).

59. condition rank.

61. I would not so! Ferdinand, unlike Antonio and Sebastian, has no ambition to be King if it means the death of Alonso.

62–3. suffer . . . mouth allow a blow-fly to foul my lips (by laying its eggs on my lips).

63. my soul i.e. my love for you is not merely physical, or of the mind, but from my very spirit.

65. fly . . . service i.e. like a bird, or an arrow.

68. this sound i.e. my words.

69. what I profess my declaration of love.

69. kind event happy outcome.

70–1. If hollowly . . . mischief if I speak insincerely, turn the best that the future has in store for me into the worst.

72. Beyond . . . world i.e. beyond anything you can imagine.

Have I lik'd several women, never any
With so full soul, but some defect in her
Did quarrel with the noblest grace she ow'd,   45
And put it to the foil; but you, O you,
So perfect and so peerless, are created
Of every creature's best!

Miranda
                    I do not know
One of my sex; no woman's face remember,
Save, from my glass, mine own; nor have I seen   50
More that I may call men than you, good friend,
And my dear father. How features are abroad,
I am skilless of; but, by my modesty,
The jewel in my dower, I would not wish
Any companion in the world but you;   55
Nor can imagination form a shape,
Besides yourself, to like of. But I prattle
Something too wildly, and my father's precepts
I therein do forget.

Ferdinand
                    I am, in my condition,
A prince, Miranda; I do think, a king –   60
I would not so! – and would no more endure
This wooden slavery than to suffer
The flesh-fly blow my mouth. Hear my soul speak:
The very instant that I saw you, did
My heart fly to your service; there resides   65
To make me slave to it; and for your sake
Am I this patient log-man.

Miranda
                    Do you love me?

Ferdinand
O heaven, O earth, bear witness to this sound,
And crown what I profess with kind event,
If I speak true! If hollowly, invert   70
What best is boded me to mischief! I,
Beyond all limit of what else i' th' world,

73. *love, prize, honour* Ferdinand makes his absolute declaration of love. From this point the action begins to move towards its inevitable outcome, the uniting of the lovers in marriage.

74. *encounter* meeting.

75–6. *Heavens . . . between 'em* the image combines the astrological shedding of influence by the planetary gods *(rain grace)* with that of fertility *(breeds)*. The Masque in Act IV, Scene i repeats the same ideas. Miranda's weeping with joy is also a fruitful rain, expressing and nourishing love.

77–9. *that dare . . . to want* i.e. Miranda does not dare to offer him the love she wants to give him, and feels even less worthy to accept his love, without which she will die.

77–9. *to want* through lack (of it).

80–1. *And all . . . it shows* i.e. the more she tries to hide the fact that she loves him, the more obvious it becomes that she does. (The image of *bigger bulk* suggests pregnancy, following *breeds* in line 76, which is the result of love.)

82. *prompt me* inspire me.

84. *maid* unmarried.

84. *fellow* mate, equal (as wife).

85. *servant* both Ferdinand and Miranda have shown themselves to be ideal lovers in their desire to serve each other.

87. *thus humble* Perhaps Ferdinand is kneeling in front of her? Being humble is the exact opposite of pride (deadliest of the deadly sins).

91. *thousand thousand* Ferdinand wishes Miranda a million (i.e. unlimited) 'fare-thee-wells'.

Stage Direction, ***severally*** in opposite directions, Ferdinand having to carry off the log he entered with.

92–3. *So glad . . . withal* I cannot be as overjoyed at this (revelation of love) as they are, because it has taken them, but not me, by surprise.

Do love, prize, honour you.
Miranda

I am a fool
To weep at what I am glad of.
Prospero
[*Aside*]   Fair encounter
Of two most rare affections! Heavens rain grace   75
On that which breeds between 'em!
Ferdinand

Wherefore weep you?
Miranda
At mine unworthiness, that dare not offer
What I desire to give, and much less take
What I shall die to want. But this is trifling;
And all the more it seeks to hide itself,   80
The bigger bulk it shows. Hence, bashful cunning!
And prompt me plain and holy innocence!
I am your wife, if you will marry me;
If not, I'll die your maid. To be your fellow
You may deny me; but I'll be your servant,   85
Whether you will or no.
Ferdinand

My mistress, dearest;
And I thus humble ever.
Miranda

My husband, then?
Ferdinand
Ay, with a heart as willing
As bondage e'er of freedom. Here's my hand.
Miranda
And mine, with my heart in't. And now farewell   90
Till half an hour hence.
Ferdinand

A thousand thousand!

[*Exeunt* FERDINAND *and* MIRANDA *severally*]

Prospero
So glad of this as they I cannot be,

94. *book* perhaps to prepare for the impressive displays of magical power in the Banquet scene (Act III, Scene iii) and the Masque (Act IV, Scene i).

95–6. *perform/Much business appertaining* carry out a great deal in connection with this love-match (i.e. the Masque to celebrate a *contract of true love*. Act IV, Scene i, line 84).

95. *perform* hints at the Masque which Prospero is to stage, rather than perform in himself.

The lyrical dignity of this short scene that has just finished is heightened by its obvious contrast with the coarse scenes in prose which precede and follow it. The drunken behaviour and crude songs of Act II, Scene ii, and the brutish violence of Act III, scene ii are dark phases between which Act III, scene i shines like a bright jewel.

Who are surpris'd withal; but my rejoicing
At nothing can be more. I'll to my book;
For yet ere supper time must I perform   95
Much business appertaining.

[Exit]

SCENE II

The main purpose of this scene is to show the comic trio's move from from drunkenness to plans for murder. In the process their relationships with one another deteriorate: Stephano becomes not much more than a tyrant (not at all the king that he would like to imagine he is), Trinculo an envious coward, and Caliban more and more disgusted with the lack of courage and single-mindedness of his heroes. They are no real threat to Prospero, and Ariel makes fools of them. By letting the audience laugh, Shakespeare provides another break, after the delicate intensity of the scene between the two lovers, and before returning to the Alonso situation at its climax.

1. *Tell not me* perhaps Trinculo has been suggesting that Stephano ought to ration the sack (white wine) which won't last long at the rate it is being consumed. In his drunken vanity, Stephano insists on being toasted by Caliban.

2. *bear up and board 'em* drink up. The image is from sea-warfare, when about to leap onto an enemy ship.

4. *folly* freak.

6. *be brain'd like us* have brains like ours.

8. *set in thy head* unseeing, glazed.

10. *tail* bottom (compare the coarse jokes of Act II, Scene ii).

12–14. *For . . . off and on* Stephano's drunken boastfulness is shown here.

12–14. *five and thirty leagues* would be 105 miles.

12–14. *recover* reach.

15. *standard* flag-bearer.

16. *no standard* i.e. Caliban is horizontal (lying on the ground) rather than vertical (standing upright).

17. *run* run away (i.e. from the enemy in battle. The flag or standard had to be kept flying as a rallying point and to show your troops that you were still fighting.)

18. *go* walk (because they are too drunk to).

18. *lie* tell lies, or even lie down. Trinculo may again be using words in a crude way (e.g. *run*: make water, *lie*: excrete).

Scene II

Another part of the island.

[Enter CALIBAN, STEPHANO *and* TRINCULO*]*

Stephano

Tell not me – when the butt is out we will drink water,
not a drop before; therefore bear up, and board 'em.
Servant-monster, drink to me.

Trinculo

Servant-monster! The folly of this island! They say
there's but five upon this isle: we are three of them,   5
if th' other two be brain'd like us, the state totters.

Stephano

Drink, servant-monster, when I bid thee; thy eyes are
almost set in thy head.

Trinculo

Where should they be set else? He were a brave
monster indeed, if they were set in his tail.   10

Stephano

My man-monster hath drown'd his tongue in sack. For
my part, the sea cannot drown me; I swam, ere I could
recover the shore, five and thirty leagues, off and on.
By this light, thou shalt be my lieutenant,
monster, or my standard.   15

Trinculo

Your lieutenant, if you list; he's no standard.

Stephano

We'll not run. Monsieur Monster.

Trinculo

Nor go neither; but you'll lie like dogs, and yet say
nothing neither.

Stephano

Moon-calf, speak once in thy life, if thou beest a good   20
moon-calf.

Caliban

How does thy honour? Let me lick thy shoe.

24. *in case* ready to.
24. *justle* jostle, shove around (i.e. in order to provoke).
25. *debosh'd* debauched.
26–7. *coward . . . sack* i.e. drunk so much wine to give him false courage.

31. *natural* idiot, half-wit.

34. *prove* turn out to be.
34. *the next tree* i.e. will be his gallows.

36–7. *I thank . . . thee* Shakespeare's contempt of 'sucking up' to people is seen in this parody of court behaviour, and is a reminder of Act I, Scene ii, line 79.
38. *Marry, will I* indeed I will. *(Marry* is a corrupt form of 'By the Virgin Mary'.)
38. *I will stand* as Alonso's butler, Stephano perhaps remembers the way he used to have to act in the king's court.

Stage Direction. *Enter Ariel* presumably placing himself behind or near to Trinculo.

43. *jesting monkey* i.e. a meddling fool.

I'll not serve him; he is not valiant.

Trinculo

Thou liest, most ignorant monster: I am in case to
justle a constable. Why, thou debosh'd fish, thou,   25
was there ever man a coward that hath drunk so much
sack as I to-day? Wilt thou tell a monstrous lie, being
but half a fish and half a monster?

Caliban

Lo, how he mocks me! Wilt thou let him, my lord?

Trinculo

'Lord' quoth he! That a monster should be such a   30
natural!

Caliban

Lo, lo again! Bite him to death, I prithee.

Stephano

Trinculo, keep a good tongue in your head, if you
prove a mutineer – the next tree! The poor monster's
my subject, and he shall not suffer indignity.   35

Caliban

I thank my noble lord. Wilt thou be pleas'd to hearken
once again to the suit I made to thee?

Stephano

Marry will I, kneel and repeat it; I will stand, and so
shall Trinculo.

[Enter ARIEL, invisible]

Caliban

As I told thee before, I am subject to a tyrant, a   40
sorcerer, that by his cunning hath cheated me of the
island.

Ariel

Thou liest.

Caliban

        Thou liest, thou jesting monkey, thou;
I would my valiant master would destroy thee.
I do not lie.   45

Stephano

Trinculo, if you trouble him any more in's tale, by this

47. *supplant* remove, knock out.

49. *Mum* be silent ('Mum's the word').

53. *this thing* i.e.Trinculo (a mere monkey rather than a man).

56. *compass'd* achieved.
57. *party* person.

58. *yield him thee* deliver him into your hands.
59. *knock . . . head* as Jael did to the sleeping Sisera *(Judges* IV.21).To kill a sleeping person was particularly cowardly and evil (compare the plot to murder Alonso, and the murders of Duncan in *Macbeth* and old Hamlet in *Hamlet*).

61. *pied ninny* a reference to Trinculo's multi-coloured jester's clothing.
61. *scurvy patch* 'moth-eaten fool'. (Scurvy produced a patchy skin condition, and patch could also refer to the jester's costume being in patches of colour.)

65. *quick freshes* flowing fresh-water streams.

68. *stock-fish* dried cod (which had been beaten before being boiled).

hand, I will supplant some of your teeth.

Trinculo

Why, I said nothing.

Stephano

Mum, then, and no more. Proceed.

Caliban

I say, by sorcery he got this isle, 50
From me he got it. If thy greatness will
Revenge it on him – for I know thou dar'st,
But this thing dare not –

Stephano

That's most certain.

Caliban

Thou shalt be lord of it, and I'll serve thee. 55

Stephano

How now shall this be compass'd?
Canst thou bring me to the party?

Caliban

Yea, yea my lord; I'll yield him thee asleep,
Where thou mayst knock a nail into his head.

Ariel

Thou liest; thou canst not. 60

Caliban

What a pied ninny's this! Thou scurvy patch!
I do beseech thy greatness, give him blows,
And take his bottle from him. When that's gone
He shall drink nought but brine; for I'll not show
  him
Where the quick freshes are. 65

Stephano

Trinculo, run into no further danger; interrupt the
monster one word further and, by this hand, I'll turn
my mercy out o' doors, and make a stock-fish of thee.

Trinculo

Why, what did I? I did nothing. I'll go farther off.

Stephano

Didst thou not say he lied? 70

115

72–3. As you . . . another time If you like being beaten, accuse me again to my face of lying.

74–5. Out . . . too are you out of your mind as well as deaf?

75–6. This . . . do this is what drink can do to a man.

75–6. murrain cattle-disease (suitable to plague a *mooncalf*).

76–7. devil . . . fingers i.e. may you lose your fingers (for beating me).

80. Prithee . . . off presumably said to Trinculo, though possibly to Caliban if Stephano can no longer stand his *fishlike smell* of body-odour close to him.

81. after . . . too although Caliban is not *afeard* of the strange noises on the island, he shows himself cowardly in telling Stephano how to kill Prospero rather than performing the murder himself.

84. there at that time, then.

84. thou mayst brain him smash his skull in.

85, 88, 91. books Caliban stresses the importance of Prospero's volumes of magic 'art'. It is significant that he only wishes to destroy the books, not to profit by studying them.

85. log this would no doubt give Caliban particular pleasure.

86. paunch . . . stake thrust a sharpened stake into his stomach. *(Brain* and *paunch,* normally nouns, have great vigour as verbs.)

87. wezand wind-pipe.

89. sot powerless fool.

92. brave utensils fine household objects.

92. for so he calls them Caliban's limited vocabulary is again suggested: he is simply quoting Prospero in using the word *utensil* (compare *nonpareil,* line 96).

93. Which . . . withal which he will display in his house when he has one.

94. And that . . . is and that which is most seriously to be considered is.

96. nonpareil unrivalled in beauty.

97–8. Sycorax . . . she . . . she . . . Sycorax the inverted repetition of the words reinforces the contrast between pure ugliness (spiritual and physical) and pure beauty (spiritual and physical).

99. great'st does least i.e. Sycorax and Miranda are as widely separated as the two ends of any scale you choose. This sort of extreme comparison can be found elsewhere in the play, e.g. Act I, Scene ii, lines 481–2 and Act III, Scene i, lines 8–9, and contributes to making the characters 'ideal' rather than 'real', i.e. no one in real life is *all* good or *all* bad.

Ariel
> Thou liest.

Stephano
> Do I so? Take thou that. *[Beats him]* As you like this,
> give me the lie another time.

Trinculo
> I did not give the lie. Out o' your wits and hearing
> too? A pox o' your bottle! This can sack and drinking   75
> do. A murrain on your monster, and the devil take
> your fingers!

Caliban
> Ha,ha, ha!

Stephano
> Now, forward with your tale. –
> Prithee stand further off.   80

Caliban
> Beat him enough, after a little time, I'll beat him
> too.

Stephano
> Stand farther. Come, proceed.

Caliban
> Why, as I told thee, 'tis a custom with him
> I' th' afternoon to sleep, there thou mayst brain him,
> Having first seiz'd his books; or with a log   85
> Batter his skull, or paunch him with a stake,
> Or cut his wezand with thy knife. Remember
> First to possess his books, for without them
> He's but a sot, as I am, nor hath not
> One spirit to command; they all do hate him   90
> As rootedly as I. Burn but his books.
> He has brave utensils – for so he calls them –
> Which, when he has a house, he'll deck withal.
> And that most deeply to consider is
> The beauty of his daughter; he himself   95
> Calls her a nonpareil. I never saw a woman
> But only Sycorax my dam and she;
> But she as far surpasseth Sycorax
> As great'st does least.

117

100. *become* grace.
100. *warrant* assure you.
101. *brave brood* fine children. (The attraction of Miranda so far as Caliban and Stephano are concerned is wholly sexual.)
104. *viceroys* Stephano thinks in terms of show (titles). They are not going to have any subjects to rule, anyway. (Here again there is a comment implied on Antonio and Sebastian who are ambitious for positions and power.)
105. *plot* plan, idea, scheme.

108. *half-hour* a reminder of the pressure of time as events gather to a head.

113. *jocund* cheerful.
113. *troll* sing heartily, 'belt out'.
113. *the catch* the song (a part-song, with each singer in turn starting to sing, the first line as the singer before him finishes it, and so in successive lines).
114. *while-ere* a short while ago.
115. *do reason* do anything within reason.

117. *Flout . . . scout* sneer and jeer.

119. *Thought is free* a well-known saying.

Stage Direction, *tabor and pipe* the actor playing Ariel was presumably trained in this difficult act of co-ordination, tapping the basic rhythm on the side drum *(tabor)* with one hand and playing a recorder *(pipe)* with the other.

Stephano

Is it so brave a lass?

Caliban

Ay, lord, she will become thy bed, I warrant,   100
And bring thee forth brave brood.

Stephano

Monster, I will kill this man, his daughter and I will
be King and Queen – save our Graces! – and Trinculo
and thyself shall be viceroys. Dost thou
like the plot, Trinculo?   105

Trinculo

Excellent.

Stephano

Give me thy hand, I am sorry I beat thee, but while
thou liv'st, keep a good tongue in thy head.

Caliban

Within this half hour will he be asleep.
Wilt thou destroy him then?

Stephano

Ay, on mine honour.   110

Ariel

This will I tell my master.

Caliban

Thou mak'st me merry; I am full of pleasure.
Let us be jocund, will you troll the catch
You taught me but while-ere?

Stephano

At thy request, monster, I will do reason, any reason. 115
Come on, Trinculo, let us sing.

[Sings]

Flout 'em and scout 'em,
And scout 'em and flout 'em;
Thought is free.

Caliban

That's not the tune.   120

[ARIEL plays the tune on a tabor and pipe]

121–9. *What . . . mercy on us!* From the boastful bawling of the song, Stephano and Trinculo are suddenly reduced to awed silence. Wonder (lines 121–3) turns to challenge (line 124), then to fear in Trinculo (line 126), and finally to an attempt at bravado by Stephano (line 127) which crumbles into panic. Caliban is astonished at the behaviour of his hero (line 129).

122–3. *picture of Nobody* a reference to a well-known broadsheet illustration of the time depicting a man with head, arms and legs but no body.

124–5. *If thou . . . thou list* if you are a man, show yourself to be one by appearing, if you are a devil, then take any form you wish.

131. *noises* musical sounds.

133. *twangling* stringed (a word formed by a combination of 'twanging' and 'jangling', perhaps).

134. *hum* like bees, or perhaps humming birds.

134. *voices* singing.

131–9. In this lyrical, almost sad speech, Caliban is for a moment transformed from a purely animal being into a spiritual one. In so doing he symbolizes one of the central themes of the play, the power of the divine (as expressed in love and harmony) over the earthly. As in Ferdinand's speech (Act III, Scene i, lines 37–48), some of the lyricism is achieved by use of repetition *(sometimes . . . sometime, sleep . . . sleep, wak'd . . . wak'd, dreaming . . . dream)* and some by soft 's' and 'm' alliteration together with rhyming effects, *noises . . . voices, some . . . hum.*

141. *music for nothing* a characteristically mean attitude by Stephano ('something for nothing', like unearned titles) and typical perhaps of someone with no ear for music, *(That's not the tune,* says Caliban, who has an ear for music, in line 120).

142. *When Prospero is destroyed* the single-minded, if simple desire of Caliban, the savage, is contrasted with the easily-distracted 'civilized' Stephano.

144. *after* i.e. pleasure before business (the bloody business).

Stephano
What is this same?

Trinculo
This is the tune of our catch, play'd by the picture of
Nobody.

Stephano
If thou beest a man, show thyself in thy likeness, if
thou beest a devil, take't as thou list.   125

Trinculo
O, forgive me my sins!

Stephano
He that dies pays all debts. I defy thee.
Mercy upon us!

Caliban
Art thou afeard?

Stephano
No, monster, not I.   130

Caliban
Be not afeard. The isle is full of noises,
Sounds, and sweet airs, that give delight, and hurt
    not.
Sometimes a thousand twangling instruments
Will hum about mine ears, and sometime voices,
That, if I then had wak'd after long sleep,   135
Will make me sleep again; and then, in dreaming,
The clouds methought would open and show riches
Ready to drop upon me, that, when I wak'd,
I cried to dream again.

Stephano
This will prove a brave kingdom to me, where I shall   140
have my music for nothing.

Caliban
When Prospero is destroy'd.

Stephano
That shall be by and by; I remember the story.

Trinculo
The sound is going away; let's follow it, and after
do our work.   145

146. *Lead, monster* i.e. as standard-bearer and protector of his 'king'. *(Lead:* compare Act II, Scene i, line 319 and Act II, Scene ii, line 186.)

147. *lays it on* i.e. beats the drum with real urgency (and draws them like children following a recruiting band).

148. *Wilt come?* perhaps said to Caliban, who might be heading for Prospero's cell while Ariel leads them away from it, but more likely to Stephano, who is looking around for *this laborer*.

148. *I'll follow* partly because he's the least powerful of the three, but mainly for fear of being separated from Stephano and meeting a 'devil', or being left alone with his enemy, Caliban.

As the trio leave the stage at the end of this scene, we can contrast their puzzled departure with their confident exit at the end of Act II, scene ii; and we can compare it with that of the royal party at the end of Act II, scene i, going with fear and wonder into the unknown. Both groups are now beginning to *suffer a sea change.*

Stephano
    Lead, monster, we'll follow. I would I could see this
    laborer, he lays it on.
Trinculo
    Wilt come? I'll follow, Stephano.

                  [Exeunt]

SCENE III

When the clowns begin their painful journey to the stagnant pool, the royal group complete the next stage of their journey towards self-knowledge and reach the turning point of the play's action. Once Ariel has spoken to them, they are imprisoned by their guilty feelings and can only be released at the end of the play.

1. By'r lakin by our Ladykin (the Virgin Mary).
2–3. Here's . . . meanders Gonzalo compares the natural paths through the undergrowth with an artificial maze (e.g. at Hampton Court), in which there are straight paths *(forthrights)* and twisting ones *(meanders)*.

5. attach'd seized.
6. To th' dulling which deadens.
7–8. Even . . . flatterer this is the place where I will finally give up hope and keep it no longer to flatter me. (i.e. like a courtier trying to persuade me that Ferdinand is still alive). The image is (in *put off*) of the king removing his royal robe: he can no longer deceive himself that Ferdinand will one day wear it (i.e. succeed him).
10. frustrate useless.

12–13. Do not . . . t'effect don't, because of one setback, give up the plan you were determined to carry out.

13. advantage favourable opportunity.
14. throughly thoroughly.

Stage Direction, **solemn** ceremonious, formal, **strange music** perhaps hautboys (oboes) to give a supernatural effect.

Stage Direction, **on the top** in Shakespeare's theatre on the upper stage, perhaps, but more probably on the top stage or musicians' gallery above the upper stage to give the effect of a 'god' controlling this spectacular example of his art which he has conjured up.

Scene III

Another part of the island.

[Enter ALONSO, SEBASTIAN, ANTONIO, GONZALO, ADRIAN, FRANCISCO, *and others]*

Gonzalo
By'r lakin, I can go no further, sir,
My old bones ache. Here's a maze trod, indeed,
Through forth-rights and meanders! By your
    patience,
I needs must rest me.

Alonso
              Old lord, I cannot blame thee,
Who am myself attach'd with weariness   5
To th' dulling of my spirits, sit down and rest.
Even here I will put off my hope, and keep it
No longer for my flatterer, he is drown'd
Whom thus we stray to find, and the sea mocks
Our frustrate search on land. Well, let him go.   10

Antonio
[Aside to SEBASTIAN*]* I am right glad that he's so out
    of hope.
Do not, for one repulse, forgo the purpose
That you resolv'd t' effect.

Sebastian
[Aside to ANTONIO*]*   The next advantage
Will we take throughly.

Antonio
[Aside to SEBASTIAN*]*   Let it be to-night,
For, now they are oppress'd with travel, they   15
Will not, nor cannot, use such vigilance
As when they are fresh.

Sebastian
[Aside to ANTONIO*]*   I say, to-night; no more.

    [Solemn and strange music, and PROSPERO *on the*
    top, invisible. Enter several strange shapes, bringing in

20. *kind keepers* guardian angels.

21. *A living drollery* a puppet show with living, flesh-and-blood figures.

21. *Now I will believe* i.e. even the sceptical Sebastian (like Antonio: *I'll believe both,* line 24) is convinced.

22–3. *unicorns . . . phoenix* legendary, fabulous creatures, (a) the unicorn, a pure white horse with single horn, symbolized purity, and (b) the phoenix, a unique bird living in Arabia, which every five hundred years died by cremating itself and creating from its own ashes another unique phoenix, was a symbol of resurrection and hope. (It is perhaps ironical that Sebastian chooses two mythical creatures so appropriate to the central idea of the play.)

25. *what . . . credit* whatever else needs to be believed (i.e. is difficult to accept).

26. *travellers ne'er did lie* i.e. no travellers' tales, however far-fetched they might seem, were 'tall stories' (because what Antonio has witnessed is much less credible).

30. *certes* certainly.

31. *monstrous shape* unnatural appearance.

33. *generation* race.

34. *Honest* honourable.

36. *muse* wonder at.

38. *want* lack.

39. *dumb discourse* i.e speaking in actions.

a banquet, and dance about it with gentle actions of
salutations, and inviting the KING, *etc., to eat, they depart]*

Alonso
What harmony is this? My good friends, hark!
Gonzalo
Marvellous sweet music!
Alonso
Give us kind keepers, heavens! What were these?   20
Sebastian
A living drollery. Now I will believe
That there are unicorns, that in Arabia
There is one tree, the phoenix' throne, one phoenix
At this hour reigning there.
Antonio
                I'll believe both;
And what does else want credit, come to me,   25
And I'll be sworn 'tis true; travellers ne'er did lie,
Though fools at home condemn 'em.
Gonzalo
                If in Naples
I should report this now, would they believe me?
If I should say, I saw such islanders,
For certes these are people of the island,   30
Who though they are of monstrous shape yet, note,
Their manners are more gentle-kind than of
Our human generation you shall find
Many, nay, almost any.
Prospero
  [Aside]   Honest lord,
Thou hast said well; for some of you there present   35
Are worse than devils.
Alonso
            I cannot too much muse
Such shapes, such gesture, and such sound,
    expressing,
Although they want the use of tongue, a kind
Of excellent dumb discourse.

39. *Praise in departing* a proverbial expression meaning, 'Wait until you depart before praising your host's entertainment,' (i.e. things may not end as pleasantly as they have begun).

41. *stomachs* appetites (i.e. for fresh food after a long sea-journey, and after their recent exhausted wandering about the island).

42. *taste* sample.

44–6. *mountaineers . . . flesh* Gonzalo describes *goitre*, a condition affecting people living in mountainous regions where there is a lack of iodine in the water, producing heavily-swollen flesh around the neck. (They looked like bulls which have a fold of loose skin hanging from their throats.)

46–7. *such . . . breasts* i.e. the Anthropophagi, mentioned in Mandeville's book of travels (written in the 14th century), and still half-believed in during Shakespeare's time.

48. *Each . . . for one* i.e. each traveller who insured himself before departure by *putting-out* (investing) money with an insurer, on his return (provided he could prove that he had reached his destination), could claim five times the sum invested from the insurer (who kept what the traveller had 'put-out', if he did not return).

49. *Good warrant of* sure proof of.

49. *stand to* take your place at table (with perhaps a sense also of 'making a stand when', 'at bay': this point in the action is the point of no return for Alonso). Note the conclusive couplet-rhyming effect *of feed . . . last . . . feel . . . past.*

51. *Brother, my lord the Duke* brother Sebastian, and you, my Lord Antonio, Duke of Milan.

52. *do as we* probably said as a courtesy (i.e. 'eat with me, the King') but possibly cautiously (i.e. to prove that they have not poisoned the food) if he suspects a plot against himself. (See note to Act II, Scene i, line 305.)

Stage Direction, ***harpy*** Ariel's appearance as one of the Furies of classical myth, divine messengers of vengeance, contrasts with his next appearance as presenter of the gracious Masque. In this scene and in the Masque spectacular devices are used.

Stage Direction, ***claps his wings*** perhaps to conceal the table for a moment to cover the disappearance of the food by a *quaint device* (clever stage mechanism). The banquet possibly disappears into the table by means of a false top.

Prospero
  [Aside]   Praise in departing.
Francisco
  They vanish'd strangely.
Sebastian
                        No matter, since   40
  They have left their viands behind, for we have
    stomachs.
  Will't please you taste of what is here?
Alonso
                              Not I.
Gonzalo
  Faith, sir, you need not fear. When we were boys,
  Who would believe that there were mountaineers,
  Dewlapp'd like bulls, whose throats had hanging
    at 'em   45
  Wallets of flesh? or that there were such men
  Whose heads stood in their breasts? which now we
    find
  Each putter-out of five for one will bring us
  Good warrant of.
Alonso
                 I will stand to, and feed,
  Although my last; no matter, since I feel   50
  The best is past. Brother, my lord the Duke,
  Stand to, and do as we.

    [Thunder and lightning. Enter ARIEL, *like a harpy; claps
    his wings upon the table; and, with a quaint device, the
                  banquet vanishes]*

53. *three men of sin* an unholy trio.

53–6. *whom . . . up you* whom Fate, which uses for its purposes this earth and all that it contains, has made the ocean, greedy as it is, to spew you up (i.e. the sea accepts everything, but you turn its stomach).

56–8. *and on . . . to live* i.e. Destiny has marooned you on this desert island (the fate accorded to uncooperative sailors).

58–60. *I have . . . selves* I have driven you out of your minds, and you are now behaving in the reckless manner of men who will stop at nothing, even at killing themselves. (In *hang* and *drown* there is a reminder of the Boatswain, Act I, Scene i, perhaps.)

Stage Direction. ***draw their swords*** this action reminds us of Ferdinand's response to Prospero (Act I, Scene ii, lines 466–74), but the reasons for the actions are very different.

61–2. *elements . . . temper'd* i.e. Ariel and his colleagues are composed of the 'spiritual' elements of air and fire, the *means* by which the *material* of the swords (earth) were tempered (forged). Their swords can no more wound the winds or kill the waves than they can harm Ariel physically.

63. *loud winds* accusing voices of the winds.

64. *still-closing* always closing up again (with perhaps the sense of closing-in for the kill as vengeful waters pouring scorn on the wild stabbing thrusts of their cornered prey).

65. *dowie* feather.

65. *plume* crest (i.e. part of his Harpy's helmet or head-dress).

66. *like* in the same way.

67. *massy* heavy. (Ariel 'freezes' them into immobility just as Prospero did Ferdinand.)

71. *sea . . . requit it* the sea has paid you back for the deed (when you exposed Prospero and Miranda to drowning).

74. *Incens'd* enraged.

74. *all the creatures* all created beings, all creation.

75. *peace* both 'inner peace of mind and spirit', and also the sense of physical peace (in that they are like kingdoms being invaded by avenging *powers,* as at the end of *Macbeth* when *the powers above Put on their instruments* in support of the soldiers waging their crusading war against Macbeth).

76. *pronounce* i.e. judgment. Ariel's speech is that of a law-court, in which the three guilty men are charged and sentenced.

77. *Ling'ring perdition* drawn-out sense of loss (of Ferdinand). (With perhaps the idea also that Alonso will be 'lost' and forgotten by the world in his long imprisonment, serving his life sentence.)

77–8. *worse . . . at once* worse than immediate execution.

Ariel

You are three men of sin, whom Destiny,
That hath to instrument this lower world
And what is in't, the never-surfeited sea   55
Hath caus'd to belch up you; and on this island
Where man doth not inhabit – you 'mongst men
Being most unfit to live. I have made you mad;
And even with such-like Valour men hang and
    drown
Their proper selves.

      [ALONSO, SEBASTIAN *etc., draw their swords*]

                You fools! I and my fellows   60
Are ministers of Fate; the elements
Of whom your swords are temper'd may as well
Wound the loud winds, or with bemock'd-at stabs
Kill the still-closing waters, as diminish
One dowle that's in my plume; my fellow-ministers   65
Are like invulnerable. If you could hurt,
Your swords are now too massy for your strengths
And will not be uplifted. But remember –
For that's my business to you – that you three
From Milan did supplant good Prospero;   70
Expos'd unto the sea, which hath requit it,
Him, and his innocent child; for which foul deed
The pow'rs, delaying, not forgetting, have
Incens'd the seas and shores, yea, all the creatures,
Against your peace. Thee of thy son, Alonso,   75
They have bereft; and do pronounce by me
Ling'ring perdition, worse than any death

78. *step by step* a reminder of Nemesis, the classical figure of vengeance sent by the gods to punish offenders, who hobbled slowly but inexorably after her victims.

78. *attend* wait upon you like attendants at court. (Ariel uses the word with fine irony: this is not the sort of attention' Alonso wants to have.)

79. *your ways* wherever you may go, till the end of your days. The image of wandering – like the Jew or like Cain with the mark of his brother's murder on his brow – repeats that of their *maze trod* through the labyrinthine paths of the island.

79–82. *whose wraths . . . ensuing* there is nothing to protect you from the wrath of the avenging powers, which would otherwise descend upon your heads here in this remote desert island, except by accepting your guilt, and by living a faultless life in the future.

Stage Direction, *thunder* Ariel disappears as he came, to discordant and dramatic thunder. By contrast, the strange *shapes* remove the table to soft music (perhaps now felt to be mocking them as it accompanies the *shapes* who now use *mocks and mows*, grinning grimaces, in place of their previous *gentle actions of salutation*).

83. *Bravely* splendidly.

84. *a grace it had, devouring* an absorbing elegance.

85. *bated* left out.

86. *hadst to say* Prospero, the 'producer', has given Ariel a part to learn and to play.

87. *observation strange* unusual precision (in following my instructions).

87. *meaner* lesser, lower.

88. *several kinds have done* have played their particular parts.

88. *high* great.

89. *knit up* bound up.

94–5. Only the *three men of sin* have heard Ariel's words, and Gonzalo is horrified at his master's frenzied expression.

95. *it is monstrous* i.e. his sin (crime against Prospero) is horribly unnatural.

96–9. *billows* waves.

98–9. *deep . . . Prosper* a fine line and a half of expressive alliteration and assonance.

98–9. *dreadful* awe-inspiring.

98–9. *pronounc'd* compare line 76.

99. *bass my trespass* i.e. the thunder in uttering *(pronounced)* Prospero's name supplied the bass notes, or musical 'ground' to the whole harmony of natural sounds which are declaring Alonso's guilt *(trespass)*.

Can be at once, shall step by step attend
You and your ways; whose wraths to guard you
    from –
Which here, in this most desolate isle, else falls   80
Upon your heads – is nothing but heart's sorrow,
And a clear life ensuing.

*[He vanishes in thunder; then, to soft music, enter the
shapes again, and dance, with mocks and mows, and
carrying out the table]*

Prospero
Bravely the figure of this harpy hast thou
Perform'd, my Ariel, a grace it had, devouring.
Of my instruction hast thou nothing bated   85
In what thou hadst to say; so, with good life
And observation strange, my meaner ministers
Their several kinds have done. My high charms
    work,
And these mine enemies are all knit up
In their distractions. They now are in my pow'r;   90
And in these fits I leave them, while I visit
Young Ferdinand, whom they suppose is drown'd,
    And his and mine lov'd darling.

[Exit above]

Gonzalo
I' th' name of something holy, sir, why stand you
In this strange stare?
Alonso
                    O, it is monstrous, monstrous!   95
Methought the billows spoke, and told me of it;
The winds did sing it to me; and the thunder,
That deep and dreadful organ-pipe, pronounc'd
The name of Prosper; it did bass my trespass.

100. *Therefore* for this reason (i.e. Alonso's crime).

101. This suicidal line of Alonso's is almost identical with Prospero's in Act V, Scene i, line 56, but also in direct contrast to it: whereas Alonso is in despair and wishes to bury the past by dying, Prospero is burying the past in the hope of a better future.

101. *e'er plummet sounded* than any ship's lead-line ever descended in measuring the depths of water.

100–2. *bedded . . . sounded . . . mudded* these three 'dead' (-ded) endings express a hopeless finality.

103. *I'll fight . . . o'er* I'll fight their legions one after the other. (Compare Stephano's reaction in Act III, Scene ii, line 127.)

104. *desperate* frantic, reckless.

105. *Like . . . after* i.e. a poison with a delayed action (like a time-bomb) which did its work long after being given to a victim. (The poison simile is apt in that Italy was generally considered the place for sophisticated drugs and poisons at the time.)

106. *bite the spirits* prick their conscience. (This image is reversed in Act II, Scene ii, line 10, where Prospero's spirits *bite* Caliban.)

108. *ecstasy* madness.

The tension of the play has been increasing as each of the three situations has brought its part of the plot to a climax. The violent and stormy conclusion to the scene, and Alonso's departure to seek Ferdinand in the sea remind us of the tempest and the abandoning of the ship with which the play began. So, the calm harmonies of the Masque in Act IV come as a relief, bringing a restoration of order which is a foreshadow of what is to come as the play ends.

Therefore my son i' th' ooze is bedded; and 100
I'll seek him deeper than e'er plummet sounded,
And with him there lie mudded.

[Exit]

Sebastian

But one fiend at a time,
I'll fight their legions o'er.
Antonio

I'll be thy second.

[Exeunt SEBASTIAN *and* ANTONIO*]*

Gonzalo

All three of them are desperate, their great guilt,
Like poison given to work a great time after, 105
Now gins to bite the spirits. I do beseech you,
That are of suppler joints, follow them swiftly,
And hinder them from what this ecstasy
May now provoke them to.
Adrian

Follow, I pray you.

[Exeunt]

ACT IV, SCENE I

In Act IV Prospero begins to return to the foreground of the action: the royal group are safely *knit up in their distractions* and the comic trio are in the stagnant pool. He can afford time for an interlude during which he presents his Masque as a betrothal celebration for Ferdinand and Miranda and as a fine exhibition of his magical powers shortly before he relinquishes them. The short episode at the end of the Act, in which Caliban and his confederates are exposed, provides a relaxation from the serious level of action, a coming down to earth from the rarefied atmosphere of the Masque before rising again to the high poetry of the confrontation of Prospero and his enemies in Act V.

1. *too austerely punished* 'treated you too harshly' (in testing him).

3. *third* possibly a misprint in the Folio edition for 'thrid' (thread). Miranda being one of the essential strands in his beings. If it is *third*, then perhaps Milan and Prospero himself are the other two thirds.

5. *tender* offer.

5. *vexations* troubles, afflictions. (The word suggests turbulent agitation of minds and waters, as in Act I, Scene ii, line 229 *still-vex'd Bermoothes*, and of the mind as in Act IV, Scene i, line 157.)

7. *strangely* wonderfully well.

8. *ratify* confirm, bless (perhaps by placing Miranda's hand in Ferdinand's and holding both in his).

9. *boast her* off praise her highly.

11. *halt* come limping along (well behind her in the 'race' in which she will *outstrip*, or leave behind, anything which tries to keep up with her – in this case, praise).

12. *Against an oracle* against a declaration by an infallible source of truth to the contrary. (The most famous of oracles was the Delphic Oracle in Ancient Greece, to which people went to receive inspired utterance from the Pythia, a priestess of Apollo, god of wisdom.)

13–14. *gift* Ferdinand is given Miranda as a rich gift (i.e. a dowry in herself) by Prospero because he has deserved to acquire her: he has earned the right to possess her by worthily standing the test imposed on him.

15. *break . . . knot* go to bed with her, take away her virginity. (*Virginknot:* the girdle worn by maidens before marriage, in ancient times.) King James's view of the importance of chastity can be seen in a sentence from his *Basi-likon Doron* (1599), a treatise on the arts of government: 'Be not ashamed then, to keepe cleane your body, which is the Temple of the holy Spirit.'

16. *sanctimonious* holy, sacred.

ACT FOUR
Scene I

Before Prospero's cell.

[*Enter* PROSPERO, FERDINAND, *and* MIRANDA]

Prospero
  If I have too austerely punish'd you,
  Your compensation makes amends, for I
  Have given you here a third of mine own life,
  Or that for which I live, who once again
  I tender to thy hand. All thy vexations   5
  Were but my trials of thy love, and thou
  Hast strangely stood the test; here, afore heaven,
  I ratify this my rich gift. O Ferdinand!
  Do not smile at me that I boast her off,
  For thou shalt find she will outstrip all praise,   10
  And make it halt behind her.
Ferdinand
                    I do believe it
  Against an oracle.
Prospero
  Then, as my gift, and thine own acquisition
  Worthily purchas'd, take my daughter. But
  If thou dost break her virgin-knot before   15
  All sanctimonious ceremonies may
  With full and holy rite be minister'd,

18–19. No sweet . . . grow there are two interwoven ideas here: (a) the heavens (gods) will only bless the marriage and make it honourably fruitful if the proper ritual is observed, and (b) the heavens (skies) will only send fertilizing showers to produce a fruitful crop if the proper ritual is observed.

18. aspersion sprinkling (a) of dew, (b) in the Catholic ritual of the 'asperges', when the holy water is sprinkled. **19. contract** betrothal.

19. barren hate referring (a) to the hateful barrenness of the soil, (b) hatred of each other for not being able to produce children.

20. Sour-ey'd bitter looks of *disdain:* anger, scorn.

20–1. bestrew . . . weeds referring both to the weeds which will spring up in place of a fruitful crop, and to the strewing of a marriage-bed with flowers (i.e. instead of a bridal bed being 'decked' with flowers to signify sweet fruit-fulness it will be strewn with weeds, sour and unfruitful).

22–3. Therefore . . . light you Therefore be careful to restrain yourselves, if you hope to receive the blessing of the god of marriage.

23. Hymen Roman god of marriage, depicted bearing a torch.

24. fair issue fine children (i.e. not malformed like Caliban).

26. opportune convenient.

26. suggestion temptation.

27. Our worser genius can my evil spirit can offer. (A reference to the idea that each human soul had a good angel and a bad angel, the latter being its *worser genius,* fighting for possession of it.)

27–8. shall . . . lust shall never reduce my honourable intentions to mere animal passion.

28–9. to take . . . celebration so that the keen pleasure of my wedding-day is reduced.

30–1. When . . . below when I shall imagine that the sun-god's chariot horses have gone lame, or that night has been chained in its dungeon below the world (i.e. Ferdinand in his eagerness for his nuptial night will think that the day is never going to end or the night to begin).

32. Sit, then i.e. like the royal couple they are, at a royal entertainment (e.g. a play or a masque in the Banqueting Hall of Whitehall).

32. talk with her presumably so that they are absorbed in each other while Prospero speaks to Ariel, (compare also Act III, Scene i, lines 57–9 when Miranda speaks of her father's *precept* not to speak too much to Ferdinand). They are silenced by Prospero at line 59 (see note).

33. What Come here!

35. meaner fellows lesser companions.

No sweet aspersion shall the heavens let fall
To make this contract grow; but barren hate,
Sour-ey'd disdain, and discord, shall bestrew   20
The union of your bed with weeds so loathly
That you shall hate it both. Therefore take heed,
As Hymen's lamps shall light you.

Ferdinand

                 As I hope
For quiet days, fair issue, and long life,
With such love as 'tis now, the murkiest den,   25
The most opportune place, the strong'st suggestion
Our worser genius can, shall never melt
Mine honour into lust, to take away
The edge of that day's celebration,
When I shall think or Phoebus' steeds are founder'd   30
Or Night kept chain'd below.

Prospero

              Fairly spoke.
Sit, then, and talk with her; she is thine own.
What, Ariel! my industrious servant, Ariel!

[Enter ARIEL]

Ariel

What would my potent master? Here I am
Prospero
Thou and thy meaner fellows your last service   35
Did worthily perform; and I must use you

37. *trick* pageant-device (i.e. comparable with that of the banquet-scene).

37. *rabble* inferior spirits.

39. *Incite them to quick motion* make them get a move on.

41. *vanity* trifling exhibition (i.e. perhaps in comparison with the demonstration of power in raising the storm).

42. *Presently?* immediately?

43. *twink* twinkling of an eye.

46. *tripping* lightly dancing.

47. *mop and mow* presumably these grimaces would be in contrast to the sneering ones of Act III, Scene iii, p 151 (stage direction).

50. *I conceive* I understand, 'I get you'.

51. *true* i.e. to your promise (to be restrained).

51. *dalliance* love-making.

52. *Too much the rein* too much freedom, too little restraint.

52–3. *oaths . . . blood* the most solemn vows are as inflammable as straw when burning passion rages between two people.

55–6. *The white . . . liver* either (a) Miranda's chaste maidenly white breast leaning upon my chest calms my passions, or (b) the pure image of the virginal Miranda in my heart cools my heated passion. (Both images are simultaneously possible.)

57. *corollary* extra spirits (i.e. too many rather than too few).

58. *pertly* briskly, promptly.

59. *No . . . silent* i.e. so that the spell of the magical Masque will not be broken.

Stage Direction. *Enter Iris* Iris was the classical literature goddess of the rainbow and messenger of the gods and symbolized peace. As the rainbow she links Juno (Queen of Heaven) with Ceres (Queen of Earth).

In such another trick. Go bring the rabble,
O'er whom I give thee pow'r, here to this place.
Incite them to quick motion; for I must
Bestow upon the eyes of this young couple   40
Some vanity of mine art; it is my promise,
And they expect it from me.

Ariel

                Presently?

Prospero

Ay, with a twink.

Ariel

Before you can say 'come' and 'go,'
And breathe twice, and cry 'so, so,'   45
Each one, tripping on his toe,
Will be here with mop and mow.
Do you love me, master? No?

Prospero

Dearly, my delicate Ariel. Do not approach
Till thou dost hear me call.

Ariel

             Well! I conceive.   50

[Exit]

Prospero

Look thou be true; do not give dalliance
Too much the rein, the strongest oaths are straw
To th' fire i' th' blood. Be more abstemious,
Or else good night your vow!

Ferdinand

            I warrant you, sir,
The white cold virgin snow upon my heart   55
Abates the ardour of my liver.

Prospero

          Well!
Now come, my Ariel, bring a corollary,
Rather than want a spirit; appear, and pertly.
No tongue! All eyes! Be silent.

[Soft music. Enter IRIS*]*

60. *bounteous* generous, liberal.

60. *leas* meadows.

61. *vetches* small cattle-fodder vegetable.

61. *pease* peas.

63. *meads* meadows.

63. *stover* winter cattle-fodder.

64. *pioned and twilled* probably a description of banks dug by pioneers (i.e. diggers, trenchers) who then 'twill' the 'brims', i.e. strengthen the top edges by revetting or lining them with criss-crossed branches.

65. *hest* command.

66. *cold . . . crowns* the fresh-water spirits (of the full streams of spring-time) have maidens' coronets made of *pioned and twili'd brims*.

66. *broom groves* some editors read 'brown groves' (i.e. shady), though a sulking lover could possibly hide among broom (gorse) bushes growing in *groves*.

68. *lass-lorn* rejected by his sweetheart.

68. *pole-dipt* probably 'poll-dipt', i.e. pollarded or pruned grape-vines in the spring.

69. *sea-marge* coastline, at the margin or edge of the sea.

69. *sterile* i.e. in contrast to the images of potential fertility in the previous lines.

70. *air* Ceres 'take the air' at the edge of the land, refreshes herself at the seaside.

70. *Queen o' th' sky* Juno.

71. *wat'ry arch* rainbow.

72. *these* i.e. your domain (described in Iris's speech).

74. *peacocks* peacocks were sacred to Juno (as doves were to Venus, see line 94), and drew her chariot.

74. *amain* swiftly.

Stage Direction. *Juno descends* either from the Heavens, the projecting roof over the apron stage of the public playhouse, in which case she would be lowered by machinery, or from the raised level of the rear stage if at an indoor performance. In either case the movement is slow since she does not reach the main stage until line 100.

Stage Direction. *Approach . . . entertain* Iris, like a royal harbinger, precedes her sovereign lady, Juno, and summons the lesser deity, Ceres, to await her monarch's arrival (as an Elizabethan noble might wait on his land to greet and entertain his Queen during one of her 'progresses').

77. *saffron* orange-red.

78. *Diffusest honey drops* spreads sweet rain-drops.

Iris

    Ceres, most bounteous lady, thy rich leas   60
    Of wheat, rye, barley, vetches, oats, and pease,
    Thy turfy mountains, where live nibbling sheep,
    And flat meads thatch'd with stover, them to keep,
    Thy banks with pioned and twilled brims,
    Which spongy April at thy hest betrims,   65
    To make cold nymphs chaste crowns; and thy
        broom groves,
    Whose shadow the dismissed bachelor loves,
    Being lass-lorn; thy pole-dipt vineyard;
    And thy sea-marge, sterile and rocky-hard,
    Where thou thyself dost air – the Queen o' th' sky,   70
    Whose wat'ry arch and messenger am I,
    Bids thee leave these, and with her sovereign grace,
    Here on this grass-plot, in this very place,
    To come and sport. Her peacocks fly amain.

    *[*JUNO *descends in her car. Approach, rich* CERES, *her to*
        entertain. Enter CERES*]*

Ceres

    Hail, many-coloured messenger, that ne'er   75
    Dost disobey the wife of Jupiter,
    Who, with thy saffron wings, upon my flow'rs
    Diffusest honey drops, refreshing show'rs;
    And with each end of thy blue bow dost crown

79–81. *And with . . . scarf i.e.* one end of the rainbow rests upon Ceres's shrubbed or wooded *(bosky)* land, and the other upon her bare uplands, like a richly-coloured scarf.

82. *short-grassed green* perhaps not simply suggesting a lawn, but also a reference to the green-baize covering of the floor of the inner stage at Whitehall.

84. *estate* bestow.

85. *heavenly bow* rainbow.

87–90. *Since . . . forsworn* since they (Venus, goddess of sexual love, and her blind son, Cupid) devised the plan by which dark Dis (Pluto, King of the Underworld, or Hades) seized my daughter Persephone (Proserpine) to be his bride, I have given up having anything to do with such a notorious pair (i.e. as Venus and Cupid).

90. *Of her society* of her company, (i.e. of meeting her).

92. *Paphos* chief shrine to Venus (a town in Cyprus).

93–6. *Here . . . lighted* i.e. Venus and Cupid have withdrawn, defeated, having thought to lure Ferdinand and Miranda (by means of a *wanton charm* = lascivious spell) to break the vow they took to remain chaste, and not sleep together before their wedding-night.

97. *Mars's hot minion* i.e. Venus, the lustful mistress of Mars, the god of war.

97. *is return'd again* has gone back to Paphos.

98. *waspish-headed son* i.e. Cupid, whose arrows sting waspishly, peevishly.

98. *broke his arrows* i.e. in a fit of temper because chastity has triumphed.

99. *sparrows* sacred to Venus; and like her doves, symbolizing amorousness and lechery.

100. *a boy right out* simply a boy.

100. *of State* stately.

101. *gait* the way she walks (i.e. in a stately manner).

102. *Go with me* Juno, protector of married couples, goes to bless the engaged couple with spiritual gifts, and Ceres to bless them with material ones.

104. *issue* children.

My bosky acres and my unshrubb'd down,   80
Rich scarf to my proud earth – why hath thy Queen
Summon'd me hither to this short-grass'd green?

Iris

A contract of true love to celebrate,
And some donation freely to estate
On the blest lovers.

Ceres

           Tell me, heavenly bow,   85
If Venus or her son, as thou dost know,
Do now attend the Queen? Since they did plot
The means that dusky Dis my daughter got,
Her and her blind boy's scandal'd company
I have forsworn.

Iris

           Of her society   90
Be not afraid. I met her Deity
Cutting the clouds towards Paphos, and her son
Dove-drawn with her. Here thought they to have done
Some wanton charm upon this man and maid,
Whose vows are that no bed-rite shall be paid   95
Till Hymen's torch be lighted; but in vain.
Mars's hot minion is return'd again;
Her waspish-headed son has broke his arrows,
Swears he will shoot no more, but play with
    sparrows,
And be a boy right out.

[JUNO alights]

Ceres

           Highest Queen of State,   100
Great Juno, comes; I know her by her gait.

Juno

How does my bounteous sister? Go with me
To bless this twain, that they may prosperous be,
And honour'd in their issue.

[They sing]

107. *still* ever, always.

109. *foison* abundance.
109. *increase* produce, crops.
110. *garners* granaries, barns for grain.
105–12. Juno's words are largely abstract (e.g. *honour, riches, marriage-blessing, continuance, joys, blessings'*) as suits her spiritual role; Ceres' are concrete (e.g. *earth, foison, barns, garners, vines, bunches, plants*) to suit her material role.
113–14. *Spring . . . harvest* Ceres has given a vision of Golden Age abundance, and now imagines Spring immediately following the late-summer harvest so that the lovers will experience no winter in their paradisal happiness. (This would always happen if Dis had not carried off Persephone and so brought winter into the world. See line 88.)
116. *so* to this end.
118. *Harmonious charmingly* music has cast its spell *(charmingly: i.e. as* a charm) upon the ear just as the spectacular *vision* has upon the eye.

122. *a wonder'd father* (a) an amazing father (i.e. to be wondered at), (b) a father capable of working wonders.
122. *and a wise wise* provides a rhyme for *Paradise*, but may be a misprint for 'wife', in which case Miranda (*O you wonder.* Act I, Scene ii, line 427) completes the picture of an Eden-island, with God-the-Father-Prospero, Adam-Ferdinand, and Eve-Miranda.

125. *There's . . . to do* there's more about to happen.
126. *marr'd* spoilt.
127. *Naiads* water-nymphs.
127. *windring* a combination of 'winding' and 'wandering'.
128. *sedg'd* reedy, with rushes growing.
129. *crisp* rippled.
129. *this green land* see note to line 82.

Juno

    Honour, riches, marriage-blessing,   105
    Long continuance, and increasing,
    Hourly joys be still upon you!
    Juno sings her blessings on you.

Ceres

    Earth's increase, foison plenty,
    Barns and garners never empty;   110
    Vines with clust'ring bunches growing,
    Plants with goodly burden bowing;
    Spring come to you at the farthest,
    In the very end of harvest!
    Scarcity and want shall shun you,   115
    Ceres' blessing so is on you.

Ferdinand

    This is a most majestic vision, and
    Harmonious charmingly. May I be bold
    To think these spirits?

Prospero

                Spirits, which by mine art
    I have from their confines call'd to enact   120
    My present fancies.

Ferdinand

             Let me live here ever;
    So rare a wonder'd father and a wise
    Makes this place Paradise.

    [JUNO and CERES whisper and send IRIS on employment]

Prospero

              Sweet now, silence;
    Juno and Ceres whisper seriously.
    There's something else to do; hush, and be mute,   125
    Or else our spell is marr'd.

Iris

    You nymphs, call'd Naiads, of the wind'ring brooks,
    With your sedg'd crowns and ever harmless looks,
    Leave your crisp channels, and on this green land
    Answer your summons, Juno does command.   130

131. *temperate* chaste, cool.

133–9. *sun-burnt sicklemen* etc. the hot and earthy male reapers meet (*encounter* often has sexual connotations in Shakespeare) the chaste nymphs in a rustic dance *(country footing)*, a fertility ritual. In the meeting of April nymphs (see line 65) and August harvesters, water and earth, and Spring and late-Summer harvest, are united.

Stage Direction, ***starts*** seems startled, alarmed.
Stage Direction, ***hollow*** reverberating.
Stage Direction, ***heavily*** sadly, mournfully.

141. *avoid* 'away with you!' (spoken to Juno, Iris, Ceres).

142. *passion* powerful emotion, anger.
143. *works* moves, disturbs, (he is 'getting worked up').

144. *distemper'd* vexed, upset (out of an even temper).
145. *in a mov'd sort* troubled, diconcerted.
147. *revels* entertainment.
148. *As I foretold you* presumably Prospero both promised (see line 41) and *foretold* between the end of Act III, Scene i, and the beginning of Act IV.
150. *baseless fabric* cloth which has no 'base' or 'ground' and therefore no substantiality.
150–5. *this vision* Prospero describes the transcience of human beings, their most splendid and apparently permanent achievements, and the world itself, in terms of actors, masque scenery, and pageant equipment which is dismantled and disappears after the performance.
153. *all which it inherit* everything which this vision possesses.

Come, temperate nymphs, and help to celebrate
A contract of true love; be not too late.

[Enter certain NYMPHS]

You sun-burnt sicklemen, of August weary,
Come hither from the furrow, and be merry;
Make holiday; your rye-straw hats put on,   135
And these fresh nymphs encounter every one
In country footing.

[Enter certain REAPERS, properly habited, they join
with the nymphs in a graceful dance; towards the end
whereof PROSPERO starts suddenly, and speaks; after
which, to a strange, hollow, and confused noise,
they heavily vanish]

Prospero
[Aside] I had forgot that foul conspiracy
Of the beast Caliban and his confederates
Against my life; the minute of their plot   140
Is almost come. [To the SPIRITS] Well done; avoid; no
    more!
Ferdinand
This is strange; your father's in some passion
That works him strongly.
Miranda
                          Never till this day
Saw I him touch'd with anger so distemper'd.
Prospero
You do look, my son, in a mov'd sort,   145
As if you were dismay'd, be cheerful, sir.
Our revels now are ended. These our actors,
As I foretold you, were all spirits, and
Are melted into air, into thin air,
And, like the baseless fabric of this vision,   150
The cloud-capp'd towers, the gorgeous palaces,
The solemn temples, the great globe itself,
Yea, all which it inherit, shall dissolve,

WILLIAM SHAKESPEARE

154. *this . . . pageant* this masque, which is pure illusion.
155. *not a rack* no trace (literally, not a cloud). There is a suggestion of 'stage-clouds' (i.e. scenery).
155. *stuff* material (perhaps connecting *with fabric* in line 150).
156. *on* of.
157. *rounded* rounded off, completed (perhaps 'brought full circle'), crowned.
157. *vex'd* agitated.
158. *weakness* i.e. that I should be so upset, not better able to control my feelings (of anger at the *foul conspiracy*).
162. *beating* i.e. agitated, restless (like the sea beating on the shore), pulsating. (Compare Act I, Scene ii, line 176.)

164. *I cleave to* I cling to, am inseparably part of.
165. *meet with* (a) confront, (b) settle our account with, (c) deal with.
166. *When . . . Ceres* either (a) when I represented (i.e. acted the part of) Ceres, or (b) when I introduced Ceres in the masque (perhaps himself playing Iris).
169. *varlets* rascals, knaves.
171. *valour* 'Dutch courage' (i.e. given them by the wine).
173. *kissing . . . feet* a reminder of Caliban prostrating himself before Stephano in Act II, Scene ii, line 146–7, *I'll kiss thy foot*. (In smiting the air and beating the ground, they are behaving like irrational tyrants cruelly maltreating their subjects, some for simply daring to breathe in their presence and others for humbly seeking their favour in submissively kissing their feet.)
173. *bending* directing their course, heading for.
174. *project* purpose, objective (compare Act V, Scene i, line 1).
174. *unback'd* unbroken, never ridden.
175–6. *prick'd . . . Advanc'd . . . lifted up* all three words mean much the same thing and exactly describe the action: first, the three 'animals' hear the drum, cocking their ears; then they look up to see where the sound is coming from; then they raise their muzzles as if to scent it. (Ariel probably imitates their actions throughout this graphic speech, as he does in true Messenger (or commentator) fashion in his other descriptions.)
178. *calf-like* perhaps a reminder of the *mooncalf*.
178. *lowing* Ariel's music was to them in their animal state like the mooing of the mother cow calling to them to follow her.

And, like this insubstantial pageant faded,
Leave not a rack behind. We are such stuff   155
As dreams are made on, and our little life
Is rounded with a sleep. Sir, I am vex'd;
Bear with my weakness, my old brain is troubled;
Be not disturb'd with my infirmity.
If you be pleas'd, retire into my cell   160
And there repose; a turn or two I'll walk
To still my beating mind.

Ferdinand and Miranda

We wish your peace.

[Exeunt]

Prospero

Come, with a thought. I thank thee, Ariel; come.

[Enter ARIEL*]*

Ariel

Thy thoughts I cleave to. What's thy pleasure?

Prospero

Spirit,
We must prepare to meet with Caliban.   165

Ariel

Ay, my commander. When I presented Ceres,
I thought to have told thee of it; but I fear'd
Lest I might anger thee.

Prospero

Say again, where didst thou leave these varlets?

Ariel

I told you, sir, they were red-hot with drinking,   170
So full of valour that they smote the air
For breathing in their faces; beat the ground
For kissing of their feet; yet always bending
Towards their project. Then I beat my tabor,
At which like unback'd colts they prick'd their ears,   175
Advanc'd their eyelids, lifted up their noses
As they smelt music; so I charm'd their ears,
That calf-like they my lowing follow'd through

179. *goss* gorse.

181. *filthy mantled* covered with scum (filth).

182–3. *that . . . feet* so that (by disturbing the foul water) the pond smelt even worse than their feet did. (Rotting leaves at the bottom of a neglected pond create an unpleasant gas.)

170–83. The physical brutishness of the trio is vigorously conveyed by enumerating parts of the body *(faces, feet, unback'd, ears, eyelids, noses, ears, tooth'd, shins, chins, feet)* and by stressing movement *(drinking, smote, breathing, beat, kissing, bending* etc).

183. *bird* suggesting Ariel's swiftness and free flight.

184. A reminder to the audience that Ariel is only visible to Prospero.

185. *trumpery* showy materials.

186. *stale* (a) bait (literally, a decoy bird) but also perhaps (b) a whore (to lure them in her gaudy gear).

187–89. *devil, devil, all, all lost* the repetitions convey the mixture of anger and regret Prospero feels at having failed (magician as he is, he can only control the physical world) and stress his failure.

188. *Nurture* education, training, upbringing. (Without the externally imposed discipline of *nurture,* man is no more than a beast and lacking in dignity and self-control.)

188–89. *my pains . . . taken* all my efforts made out of kindness.

190. *age* with each passing year.

191. *cankers* grows more malignant, corrupted, infected with evil.

190–1. *body . . . mind* the Platonic idea that the body and the mind resemble each other is also expressed in Miranda's description of Ferdinand (Act I, Scene ii, line 458).

Stage Direction, *glistening apparel* i.e. the *trumpery* (line 185). Like children, they are attracted by bright, shining objects, and forget that 'All that glisters is not gold' *(Merchant of Venice, Act II, Scene vii, line 65).* However, since the *stuffs* came from Prospero's wardrobe, they might have been worn by him, or made up into dresses for Miranda; robes are only 'real gold' when worn by their rightful owners, otherwise they are mere show.

193. *line* either (a) clothes-line, or (b) lime-tree (see Act V, Scene i, line 10).

194. *blind mole* i.e. a creature with the most acute hearing listening just below them ('so softly that even…').

197. *play'd the Jack* (a) behaved like a knave, (b) been a misleading Jack o' Lantern, will o' th' wisp. (The will o' th' wisp, a light probably produced by marsh-gas, which led travellers astray by night and into boggy land, combines with the idea of a deceitful knave tricking them.)

Tooth'd briers, sharp furzes, pricking goss, and
    thorns,
Which enter'd their frail shins. At last I left them   180
I' th' filthy mantled pool beyond your cell,
There dancing up to th' chins, that the foul lake
O'erstunk their feet.

Prospero

                This was well done, my bird.
Thy shape invisible retain thou still.
The trumpery in my house, go bring it hither   185
For stale to catch these thieves.

Ariel

              I go, I go.

           [Exit]

Prospero

A devil, a born devil, on whose nature
Nurture can never stick; on whom my pains,
Humanely taken, all, all lost, quite lost;
And as with age his body uglier grows,   190
So his mind cankers. I will plague them all,
Even to roaring.

    [Re-enter ARIEL, *loaden with glistering apparel]*

Come, hang them on this line.

    *[*PROSPERO *and* ARIEL *remain, invisible. Enter* CALIBAN,
        STEPHANO, *and* TRINCULO, *all wet]*

Caliban

Pray you, tread softly, that the blind mole may not
Hear a foot fall; we now are near his cell.   195

Stephano

Monster, your fairy, which you say is a harmless
fairy, has done little better than play'd the Jack with
us.

199. *horse-piss* horse-urine (perhaps suggested by *stale* in line 186, which can mean urine).

202. *displeasure* i.e. 'King' Stephano will show his royal displeasure. Compare the phrase 'at the king's pleasure'. (The word may have some subconscious link for Shakespeare with evil-smelling ponds. In *All's Well* we find: *I am now, sir, muddied in fortune's mood, and smell somewhat strong of her displeasure,* and *the unclean fishpond of her displeasure.)*

204–5. These words by Caliban could in another context be just those of a cringing courtier seeking a favour of his king.

206. *hoodwink this mischance* cover up this unfortunate episode (in the pool). (Hawks were 'hoodwinked', i.e. covered with a hood, making them harmless. Caliban wants his mistake made in calling Ariel a *harmless fairy* to be forgotten.)

209. *disgrace and dishonour* both words are suitable to nobles who have suffered a defeat.

211. *That's more* perhaps this is deliberately ambiguous, i.e. Trinculo is probably referring to the loss of the bottle, but would like to be thought to refer to the loss of his honour.

213. *fetch* off rescue, get back.

213. *o'er ears totally immersed.* (Perhaps Stephano starts to leave and is stopped by Caliban, who keeps him to his purpose by pointing out that they are at the entrance to the cell.) There may be a parallel between 'King' Stephano and King Alonso here: the former going to plunge into the pond for his lost bottle, the latter into the sea for his lost son.

217. *good* mischief excellent crime. (An example of an oxymoron or paradoxical phrase.)

219. *foot-licker* Caliban is the very picture of obsequiousness. (Compare Act III, Scene ii, line 22, *lick thy fool,* and references to kissing feet. Licking is equivalent to 'sucking up' as is seen in *Hamlet,* Act III, Scene ii, line 65, *Let the candied tongue lick absurd pomp.)*

220. Stephano's pompously theatrical words show him to be no man for deeds.

222. *O King Stephano* Trinculo is not, presumably, deliberately 'taking the mickey' out of Stephano, but the allusion to the Ballad of King Stephen would underline to the audience Stephano's poor claims to kingship: *King Stephen was a worthy peer, His breeches cost him but a crown.*

Trinculo

Monster, I do smell all horse-piss at which my nose
is in great indignation.   200

Stephano

So is mine. Do you hear, monster? If I should take a
displeasure against you, look you –

Trinculo

Thou wert but a lost monster.

Caliban

Good my lord, give me thy favour still.
Be patient, for the prize I'll bring thee to   205
Shall hoodwink this mischance, therefore speak softly.
All's hush'd as midnight yet.

Trinculo

Ay, but to lose our bottles in the pool!

Stephano

There is not only disgrace and dishonour in that,
monster, but an infinite loss.   210

Trinculo

That's more to me than my wetting; yet this is your
harmless fairy, monster.

Stephano

I will fetch off my bottle, though I be o'er ears for my
labour.

Caliban

Prithee, my king, be quiet. Seest thou here,   215
This is the mouth o' th' cell; no noise, and enter.
Do that good mischief which may make this island
Thine own for ever, and I, thy Caliban,
For aye thy foot-licker.

Stephano

Give me thy hand. I do begin to have bloody 220
thoughts.

Trinculo

O King Stephano! O peer! O worthy Stephano!
Look what a wardrobe here is for thee!

Caliban

Let it alone, thou fool, it is but trash.

226. *frippery* old clothes shop.

226. *O . . . Stephano* Trinculo is no doubt parading in one of the flashier robes or pieces of material as he says this.

227. *by this hand* Stephano makes a threatening gesture (like the bully he is).

230. *dropsy drown* may this fool be drowned by the watery fluid in his own body. *dropsy* is a condition in which there is too much body fluid in a person, causing him to swell. (In *drown* there is another echo of death by water.)

231. *luggage* encumbering rubbish.

233. *crown* crown of the head (with an allusion to Stephano's royal crown, which he will usurp from Prospero).

234. *Make us strange stuff* i.e. we will be transformed by his tortures *(pinching)* into strange material *(stuff)* if we are diverted from our purpose by this *stuff*.

235–40. Stephano and Trinculo are almost certainly exchanging obscene puns, accompanied perhaps by appropriate actions.

235. *Mistress line* spoken to the lime-tree or clothes-line as he takes the jerkin. (Could he be *singing* the words. *Mistress line, is not this my jerkin?* to the tune, *O Mistress mine where are you roaming?* from *Twelfth Night?*

235. *jerkin* short jacket.

236. *under the line* (a) under the lime-tree, or (b) the clothes-line, or (c) the loin ('-oin' was pronounced '-ine' at the time), or (d) below the Equator (still referred to as 'line' in the phrase 'crossing the line').

237. *lose your hair* either (a) through fever (e.g. scurvy) contracted at the Equator, or (b) venereal disease.

238. *Do, do* 'Go on, go on!' (Either referring to Stephano's stealing, or to his succession of puns, or both.)

238. *steal* if steal is pronounced 'stale' (the '-ea' as in 'break') then Prospero's words in line 186 are recalled, and the loin-hair pun continued.

238. *by line and level* systematically. (The reference is to building, using a plumb-line for vertical and a level for horizontal accuracy, i.e. we steal according to rule'.)

238. *an't like* if it please.

242–3. *pass of pate* 'crack', witty remark (lit. a thrust of wit).

244. *lime* bird-lime (used by thieves who coated branches with this sticky substance in order to catch birds).

246. *none on't* none of it, nothing to do with it.

246. *time* opportunity.

247. *barnacles* barnacle-geese. (Popular folklore said that ship's barnacles were metamorphosed into geese. Taken with *apes* this could be another example of the general theme of transformation, in this case into something lower in the order of natural beings.)

Trinculo

O, ho, monster; we know what belongs to a   225
frippery. O King Stephano!

Stephano

Put off that gown, Trinculo; by this hand, I'll have
that gown.

Trinculo

Thy Grace shall have it.

Caliban

The dropsy drown this fool! What do you mean   230
To dote thus on such luggage? Let't alone,
And do the murder first. If he awake,
From toe to crown he'll fill our skins with pinches;
Make us strange stuff.

Stephano

Be you quiet, monster. Mistress line, is not this 235
my jerkin? Now is the jerkin under the line; now,
jerkin, you are like to lose your hair, and prove a bald
jerkin.

Trinculo

Do, do. We steal by line and level, an't like your Grace.

Stephano

I thank thee for that jest; here's a garment for't. Wit 240
shall not go unrewarded while I am king of this
country. 'Steal by line and level' is an excellent pass
of pate; there's another garment for't.

Trinculo

Monster, come, put some lime upon your fingers,
and away with the rest.   245

Caliban

I will have none on't. We shall lose our time,
And all be turn'd to barnacles, or to apes

248. *foreheads villainous low* i.e. ugly, serflike lowbrows.
Stage Direction. This episode may correspond to an Anti-masque, a spectacular yet comic, earthy contrast to the dignified and supernatural Masque.

254–6. *Mountain . . . Silver . . . Fury . . . Tyrant* the names of the hounds in Prospero's spirit-pack.

257. *charge* command.
258. *dry convulsions* cramps, spasms (thought in Shakespeare's time to be caused by a deficiency in bodily fluids needed to lubricate the joints).
259. *aged cramps* old people's cramps.
259. *pinch-spotted* bruised (black and blue) with pinching.
260. *pard* panther.
260. *cat o' mountain* leopard.

Since Act V will be largely occupied with Prospero's reconciliation with his enemies and the resignation of his Art, Shakespeare, using the device of a play within a play, gives most of Act IV to the marriage theme; for it is the lovers who are the future, and it is on them that a better life depends. The Masque, with its themes of self-control and fruitfulness, points the way to a better life.

With foreheads villainous low.

Stephano

Monster, lay-to your fingers, help to bear this away
where my hogshead of wine is, or I'll turn you out of 250
my kingdom. Go to, carry this.

Trinculo

And this.

Stephano

Ay, and this.

[A noise of hunters heard. Enter divers SPIRITS, *in shape
of dogs and hounds, hunting them about;* PROSPERO
and ARIEL *setting them on]*

Prospero

Hey, Mountain, hey!

Ariel

Silver! there it goes, Silver!   255

Prospero

Fury, Fury! There, Tyrant, there! Hark, hark!

[CALIBAN, STEPHANO, and TRINCULO are driven out]

Go charge my goblins that they grind their joints
With dry convulsions, shorten up their sinews
With aged cramps, and more pinch-spotted make them
Than pard or cat o' mountain.

Ariel

                               Hark, they roar.   260

Prospero

Let them be hunted soundly. At this hour
Lies at my mercy all mine enemies.
Shortly shall all my labours end, and thou
Shalt have the air at freedom; for a little
Follow, and do me service.   265

[Exeunt]

ACT V, SCENE I

The three strands of the plot are now gathered together; the paths trodden by the three groups meet at Prospero's cell. As *The Tempest* is not a tragedy of revenge but a romance comedy of reconciliation, Prospero performs the *rarer action* of pardoning his enemies: it is always easier to be vindictive than to forgive. In setting them free by forgiveness and releasing Ariel, he frees himself and his Art is no longer needed.

Stage Direction, *in his magic robes* the break between Acts IV and V is perhaps no longer than to allow Prospero to withdraw into his cell and reappear in his magic robes, which he has to put on in order formally to divest himself of them in the transformation during Ariel's song (lines 88–94).

1. *project* (a) undertaking, purpose, (b) 'projection', the experiment by which alchemists hoped to change base metal into gold by means of the 'philosopher's stone'. (Prospero's purpose in the play is to transform the characters and the situation with which it starts, to change them from base metal into gold.)

1. *gather to a head* (a) approach the crisis (of the experiment), (b) come to bursting-point (of a boil), when the corruption of the past will come into the open and be cleared.

2. *charms crack not* (a) spells remain unbroken, (b) the chemical retort has not exploded, ruining the experiment.

2–3. *time . . . carriage* there is little left to do. (Time is personified as someone now able to walk erect after shedding most of his burden, i.e. having discharged his duty, as Prospero has almost done.)

8. *gave in charge* instructed me.

10. *line-grove* lime-tree grove.

10. *weather-fends* shields from rough weather, storms.

11. *budge till your release* move until you release them (i.e. give the order, like a magistrate, for their release).

16–17. *like . . . reeds* like winter rain dripping rapidly and steadily from the overhanging thatch of a cottage roof (i.e. jutting out like a beard). Compare note to Act I, Scene ii, line 213.

17. *works 'em* moves them (with remorse).

18. *affections* emotions, feelings.

8–19. Ariel's descriptive speech, broken into slow, short phrases and sentences, not only persuades Prospero of his enemies' change of heart but prepares the audience to accept the transformation. Ariel's dramatic role is largely to prepare us for the next step in the action by telling Prospero of what has just happened.

ACT FIVE
Scene I

Before Prospero's cell.

[Enter PROSPERO *in his magic robes, and* ARIEL*]*

Prospero
Now does my project gather to a head;
My charms crack not, my spirits obey; and time
Goes upright with his carriage. How's the day?
Ariel
On the sixth hour; at which time, my lord,
You said our work should cease.
Prospero
            I did say so,   5
When first I rais'd the tempest. Say, my spirit,
How fares the King and 's followers?
Ariel
                  Confin'd together
In the same fashion as you gave in charge;
Just as you left them; all prisoners, sir,
In the line-grove which weather-fends your cell;   10
They cannot budge till your release. The King,
His brother, and yours, abide all three distracted,
And the remainder mourning over them,
Brim full of sorrow and dismay; but chiefly
Him you term'd, sir, 'the good old lord, Gonzalo';   15
His tears run down his beard, like winter's drops
From eaves of reeds. Your charm so strongly works
    'em
That if you now beheld them your affections
Would become tender.
Prospero
           Dost thou think so, spirit?
Ariel
Mine would, sir, were I human.

20. *And mine shall* the three simple words are highly expressive of a firm decision.

21. *a touch* a sensitive awareness, delicate sympathy

22–4. *shall not . . . thou art?* shall I, a human being like them, experiencing everything as acutely as they do, and feeling it as sensitively, not be moved with more human sympathy towards them than you are?

25. *high wrongs* great injuries done to me.

25. *struck to th' quick* the sharp sound of the words suggests the action of touching a nerve.

25. *quick* the sensitive flesh below the skin (and, taken with *struck,* also suggesting a sudden pain). There might also be a sense in which Prospero has been repeatedly lashed by their *high wrongs* so that the skin has been stripped and the tender flesh below exposed.

26–30. Prospero chooses the way of forgiveness, nobler behaviour then that of (even righteous) anger, it is a finer course of action to do positive good than to take an easier, more 'natural' revenge. His whole aim has been, he says, to 'make it up' once he was sure that they were penitent, and once he has achieved this end there will be no more need for him to show any displeasure.

33–50. Prospero's lines probably derive from Medea's incantation in Ovid's *Metamorphoses* (Book VII). Shakespeare may have worked both from the original Latin and from Golding's version, an English translation (1567). Comparison with the original shows how English Shakespeare made many of the details, from *demi-puppets* to *curfew*.

36. *demi-puppets* little elves.

37. *green sour ringlets* the 'fairy-rings' of darker grass in which toadstools grow, made by dancing fairies (according to folklore).

39–40. *midnight . . . curfew* mushrooms appear only by night and are thus like spirits at liberty to appear on earth only between curfew and cockcrow, i.e. during the hours when man is indoors.

40. *curfew* the moment when household fires had to be damped down to reduce the risk of a conflagration. Cottagers would then go to bed, and the mushrooms could prepare to come out.

41. *masters* spirits.

41. *be-dimm'd* eclipsed.

42. *call'd . . . winds* released the rebellious winds from their caves (their homes, according to classical myth, and in this context confinement from which they are set free; perhaps like mutineers). This is yet another image of release.

43. *azur'd vault* blue (over-arching) sky.

45. *fire* lightning. Possibly suggesting in *given fire,* the the *roaring war* image, the touching-off of cannon by a linstock.

Prospero

              And mine shall.   20
Hast thou, which art but air, a touch, a feeling
Of their afflictions, and shall not myself,
One of their kind, that relish all as sharply,
Passion as they, be kindlier mov'd than thou art?
Though with their high wrongs I am struck to th'
    quick,   25
Yet with my nobler reason 'gainst my fury
Do I take part, the rarer action is
In virtue than in vengeance; they being penitent,
The sole drift of my purpose doth extend
Not a frown further. Go release them, Ariel,   30
My charms I'll break, their senses I'll restore,
And they shall be themselves.

Ariel

              I'll fetch them, sir.

[Exit]

Prospero

Ye elves of hills, brooks, standing lakes, and groves;
And ye that on the sands with printless foot
Do chase the ebbing Neptune, and do fly him   35
When he comes back; you demi-puppets that
By moonshine do the green sour ringlets make,
Whereof the ewe not bites; and you whose pastime
Is to make midnight mushrooms, that rejoice
To hear the solemn curfew; by whose aid –   40
Weak masters though ye be – I have be-dimm'd
The noontide sun, call'd forth the mutinous winds,
And 'twixt the green sea and the azur'd vault
Set roaring war. To the dread rattling thunder
Have I given fire, and rifted Jove's stout oak   45
With his own bolt; the strong-bas'd promontory

45–6. *Jove's . . . bolt* Jupiter's own thunderbolt is being used against him to split his own tree, the royal oak.

47. *spurs* roots. Perhaps continuing the battle image, with horsed knights up-ended by cannon-balls and explosions.

48. *pine and cedar* i.e. both tall trees, and perhaps also chosen for the alliterative 'p' and 's' sounds, following *strong . . . promontory . . . spurs pluck'd*.

50. *rough magic* crudely material (physical) kind of magic (in contrast to the more difficult and subtle power of transforming men's minds), using the elements of fire, air, water, earth. (See note to Act I, Scene ii, lines 1–13.)

51. *abjure* renounce.

51. *requir'd* requested.

53. *mine end* my purpose.

53–4. *that . . . for* for whom rhis magical music is being played.

54. *staff* magician's wand.

54–7. *break . . . book* Prospero will render his wand useless by breaking it, and inaccessible by burying it too deep for digging up, and drown his volume of magic lore in a depth of water to the bottom of which the longest plumb-line cannot reach. No one, not even he, will be able to use them again: they will be quite dead and given respectively an earthy and watery grave.

Stage Direction, ***frantic gesture*** perhaps the *three men of sin* enter in identical postures to those they left the stage with in Act III, Scene iii.

Stage Direction, ***the circle*** drawn by Prospero with his staff.

58–9. *A solemn . . . brains* Prospero uses the accepted theory of Renaissance times that music (harmony) is the means of soothing and settling a disturbed mind (i.e. one in a discordant state).

60. *boil'd* over-heated, agitated, seethed, and perhaps with the sense of reduced, liquefied, rather than hard-boiled (like an egg within its shell).

62. *Holy* venerable. (Though lower in rank than the three men of sin, Gonzalo is the first to be greeted.)

63–4. *Mine . . . drops* my eyes, full of fellow-feeling at the sight of your weeping, shed tears of sympathy.

64. *apace* rapidly.

65. *as* just as, in the same way as.

66–8. *so . . . reason* so their returning consciousness begins to disperse the fog of incomprehension which blankets their understanding. (Compare the truth 'dawning' on us.) The image is of early-morning mists being dissolved by the rising sun creeping the horizon.

69. *true* honourable, honest.

70. *him* i.e. Alonso (towards whom Gonzalo's loyalty has been demonstrated during the play).

70–1. *pay . . . Home* reward you in full for your kindnesses.

Have I made shake, and by the spurs pluck'd up
The pine and cedar. Graves at my command
Have wak'd their sleepers, op'd, and let 'em forth,
By my so potent art. But this rough magic   50
I here abjure; and, when I have requir'd
Some heavenly music – which even now I do –
To work mine end upon their senses that
This airy charm is for, I'll break my staff,
Bury it certain fathoms in the earth,   55
And deeper than did ever plummet sound
I'll drown my book.

[Solemn music]

[Here enters ARIEL *before; then* ALONSO, *with a frantic
gesture, attended by* GONZALO; SEBASTIAN *and*
ANTONIO *in like manner, attended by* ADRIAN *and*
FRANCISCO. *They all enter the circle which* PROSPERO
had made, and there stand charm'd; which PROSPERO
observing, speaks]

A solemn air, and the best comforter
To an unsettled fancy, cure thy brains,
Now useless, boil'd within thy skull! There stand,   60
For you are spell-stopp'd.
Holy Gonzalo, honourable man,
Mine eyes, ev'n sociable to the show of thine,
Fall fellowly drops. The charm dissolves apace,
And as the morning steals upon the night,   65
Melting the darkness, so their rising senses
Begin to chase the ignorant fumes that mantle
Their clearer reason. O good Gonazalo,
My true preserver, and a loyal sir
To him thou follow'st! I will pay thy graces   70
Home both in word and deed. Most cruelly

73. *a furtherer . . . act* aided and abetted you in my usurpation.

74. *pinch'd* tormented with remorse.

74–5. *Flesh . . . mine* you, my brother, my own flesh and blood. The inversion of the natural order of words emphasizes the unnaturalness of Antonio's action by stressing *flesh and blood.*

75–6. *entertain'd . . . nature* took Ambition into your service and gave Pity and Fraternal Feeling 'the sack', (i.e. dismissed them).

75–6. *Expell'd* is also a reminder of Antonio's expulsion of Prospero.

78. *here* on this island.

78. *your* king i.e. because Antonio has subjected the coronet of Milan to the crown of Naples (see Act I, Scene ii, line 114), Alonso is his king.

79–82. *Their . . . muddy* their minds are at present like an estuary at low tide, empty, dead, mud-bound, and useless for navigation (i.e. for receiving or conveying ideas), as consciousness returns, it is like the sea flooding back until the mud-flats are covered and the estuary is once more navigable. (The seafaring image is appropriate to the play, and adds the suggestion of happy ending with a vessel returning to port on the flood-tide.)

83. *That yet . . . know me* can see me yet, or would recognize me if he could.

85. *disease me* divest myself (of my magic robes).

86. *As I was sometime Milan* as I used to look when I was formerly Duke of Milan.

88–94. *Where . . . bough* as he helps to transform Prospero, Ariel sings of his freedom. The setting, with its *bee, cowslip, owls, bat,* and *blossom,* is that of an English summer's day and night, rather than a Mediterranean one.

91–2. *fly after* follow, pursue.

96. *So, so, so* yes, that's it, fine! Prospero makes the final adjustments to his dress, with Ariel's help.

101. *presently* at once.

102. *I drink the air before me* I suck in the air in front of me (as I fly along). Ariel moves in all the elements, but as a spirit of air he lives by that element: i.e. air is 'meat and drink' to him.

Didst thou, Alonso, use me and my daughter;
Thy brother was a furtherer in the act.
Thou art pinch'd for't now, Sebastian. Flesh and
    blood,
You, brother mine, that entertain'd ambition,   75
Expell'd remorse and nature, who, with Sebastian –
Whose inward pinches therefore are most strong –
Would here have kill'd your king, I do forgive thee,
Unnatural though thou art. Their understanding
Begins to swell, and the approaching tide   80
Will shortly fill the reasonable shore
That now lies foul and muddy. Not one of them
That yet looks on me, or would know me. Ariel,
Fetch me the hat and rapier in my cell,
I will disease me, and myself present   85
As I was sometime Milan. Quickly, spirit;
Thou shalt ere long be free.

Ariel

[on returning, sings and helps to attire him]

Where the bee sucks, there suck I;
In a cowslip's bell I lie;
There I couch when owls do cry.   90
On the bat's back I do fly
After summer merrily.
Merrily, merrily shall I live now
Under the blossom that hangs on the bough.

Prospero

Why, that's my dainty Ariel! I shall miss thee;   95
But yet thou shalt have freedom. So, so, so.
To the King's ship, invisible as thou art;
There shalt thou find the mariners asleep
Under the hatches; the master and the boatswain
Being awake, enforce them to this place;   100
And presently, I prithee.

Ariel

I drink the air before me, and return
Or ere your pulse twice beat.

106. *Sir King* perhaps spoken with irony.

108–9. *For . . . body* to reassure you that I am a living prince speaking to you (and not a spirit in disguise), I embrace you physically (so that you can feel that I am flesh and blood).

112–13. *some . . . been* some magic illusion to deceive me, as I have been deceived recently (i.e. by the banquet).
115. *Th'affliction of my mind amends* my mind begins to recover from the affliction.
116–17. *This . . . story* if all this is real and I'm not just dreaming it, then it demands a most unusual explanation.
118. *Thy dukedome I resign* I release your Dukedom from any obligation to pay tribute to me.
119. *wrongs* injuries done to you (compare line 25).

120. *noble friend* Gonzalo.
121. *embrace thine age* embrace you, old man (venerable greybeard).
122. *confined* set limits to (i.e. because it is 'boundless').

123–4. *You do . . . isle* you are still experiencing some of the illusions peculiar to the island. (The banquet in Act III, Scene iii may be alluded to in *taste . . . subtleties. Subtleties* was a term used for skilfully ornamented confections made of sugar and jelly and eaten at feasts.)
125. *things certain* things to be real.
126. *brace* pretty pair (ironically contemptuous).
126. *minded* disposed, inclined.

[Exit]

Gonzalo

    All torment, trouble, wonder and amazement,
    Inhabits here. Some heavenly power guide us   105
    Out of this fearful country!

Prospero

                     Behold, Sir King,
    The wronged Duke of Milan, Prospero.
    For more assurance that a living prince
    Does now speak to thee, I embrace thy body,
    And to thee and thy company I bid   110
    A hearty welcome.

Alonso

                 Whe'er thou be'st he or no,
    Or some enchanted trifle to abuse me,
    As late I have been, I not know. Thy pulse
    Beats, as of flesh and blood; and, since I saw thee,
    Th' affliction of my mind amends, with which,   115
    I fear, a madness held me. This must crave –
    An if this be at all – a most strange story.
    Thy dukedom I resign, and do entreat
    Thou pardon me my wrongs. But how should
       Prospero
    Be living and be here?

Prospero

                 First, noble friend,   120
    Let me embrace thine age, whose honour cannot
    Be measur'd or confin'd.

Gonzalo

                Whether this be
    Or be not, I'll not swear.

Prospero

               You do yet taste
    Some subtleties o' th' isle, that will not let you
    Believe things certain. Welcome, my friends all!   125
    [Aside to SEBASTIAN *and* ANTONIO*]* But you, my brace
      of lords, were I so minded,

127. *pluck* draw, bring down.
128. *justify* prove (i.e. *traitors* because of their treasonous plot to kill Alonso).

129. *The devil speaks in him* i.e. he is a sorcerer, using black magic and being used by the devil as a mouthpiece.
129. *No* Prospero overhears the remark and refutes it.

131. *even infect* indeed contaminate.
132. *rankest* grossest and foulest. (The word is often used of weeds in Shakespeare, and suggests both size and smell.)
132. *require* demand, request (compare line 51).
134. *restore* return to me.

135. *particulars of thy preservation* details of how you managed to survive.
136. *whom* who.
138. *sharp the point* i.e. like a knife in his heart. (Compare the phrase 'prick your conscience'.)

139. *woe* sorry.

140. *patience* the personification perhaps suggests the puritan girl's name. (Compare *Temperance*, Act II, Scene i, line 42.) Alonso's sickness of spirits is beyond the skill of Mistress Patience to cure. **142–4.** *of whose . . . content* through whose gentle help (mercy) as nurse, I myself have her supreme power (to heal) in a similar condition (bereavement), and remain content (to accept the loss because she has soothed me with her nursing).

144. *the like* the same.
145. *As great to me as late* as heavy a loss as it is a recent one. (The economy of the language, with the added compactness of the rhyme *great . . . late*, is notable.)
145–7. *supportable . . . you* I have much weaker resources to make bearable the loss of a dearly-loved one than you can call upon to console you (i.e. Alonso still has Claribel, but there may also be the suggestion that a daughter is more precious to a father than a son, even).

I here could pluck his Highness' frown upon you,
And justify you traitors; at this time
I will tell no tales.

Sebastian

　　[Aside]　　　　　The devil speaks in him.

Prospero

　　　　　　　　　　　　　No.

For you, most wicked sir, whom to call brother　　130
Would even infect my mouth, I do forgive
Thy rankest fault – all of them; and require
My dukedom of thee, which perforce I know
Thou must restore.

Alonso

　　　　　　　　If thou beest Prospero,
Give us particulars of thy preservation,　　135
How thou hast met us here, whom three hours since
Were wreck'd upon this shore; where I have lost –
How sharp the point of this remembrance is! –
My dear son Ferdinand.

Prospero

　　　　　　　　I am woe for't, sir.

Alonso

Irreparable is the loss, and patience　　140
Says it is past her cure.

Prospero

　　　　　　　　I rather think
You have not sought her help, of whose soft grace
For the like loss I have her sovereign aid,
And rest myself content.

Alonso

　　　　　　　　You the like loss!

Prospero

As great to me as late; and, supportable　　145
To make the dear loss, have I means much weaker
Than you may call to comfort you, for I
Have lost my daughter.

Alonso

　　　　　　　A daughter!

149–50. *O heavens . . . there!* Alonso invokes the gods to perform a miracle (which would entail his willing resignation of the crown), and it is this that Prospero has hoped to hear him say.

151. *Myself . . . bed* Alonso would willingly be buried/drowned if Ferdinand could only thereby be resurrected. The idea of new life springing from the dead, young king from old, is an ancient and natural one, here strongly supported in suggestion by *oozy bed*, suggesting fertility.

153. *last* late, recent.

154. *admire* wonder, marvel.

154. *encounter* meeting (perhaps with the suggestion of two opposed forces or champions).

155. *devour their reason* i.e. stand open-mouthed and uncomprehending (literally, consume their powers of reason).

155–6. *scarce . . . truth* they can hardly believe their eyes (i.e. that their eyes are not deceiving them, like servants who do not carry out their duties (*offices*) honestly – (*of truth*).

157. *natural breath* words spoken by human beings.

158. *justled* jostled, shoved, (compare Act III, Scene ii, line 25).

159. *very* very same, veritable.

162. *yet* for now.

163. *chronicle of day* a long story which will need several days (to tell).

164. *relation for a breakfast* a story that can be related at a single sitting ('over the breakfast coffee').

165. *Befitting* suitable for.

167. *abroad* beyond myself. (Or he may mean around and about, beyond the immediate vicinity of his cell.)

169. *requite* repay.

170. *bring forth a wonder* produce a miracle. The re-birth of the 'lost' children is suggested by *bring forth*. In *a wonder* the miracle that both children are alive is expressed; and Miranda's name again suggested.

Stage Direction, *discovers* reveals (by drawing back the curtains of the inner stage).

Stage Direction, *playing at chess* (a) they are engaged in an aristocratic game, suitable for romantic royal lovers to play, (b) in playing chess they would be together, yet suitably separated and innocently employed.

174–5. *Yes, for . . . play* this is much disputed by editors. The meaning may be as follows: Miranda says that Ferdinand would certainly cheat her (*play me false*) if the whole world were at stake, and would even argue (*wrangle*) with her over a mere twenty kingdoms, yet in spite of this behaviour she is so much in love with him that she would still say that he was playing fairly.

O heavens, that they were living both in Naples,
The King and Queen there! That they were, I wish   150
Myself were mudded in that oozy bed
Where my son lies. When did you lose your daughter?

Prospero
In this last tempest. I perceive these lords
At this encounter do so much admire
That they devour their reason, and scarce think   155
Their eyes do offices of truth, their words
Are natural breath; but, howsoe'er you have
Been justled from your senses, know for certain
That I am Prospero, and that very duke
Which was thrust forth of Milan; who most strangely 160
Upon this shore, where you were wreck'd, was landed
To be the lord on't. No more yet of this;
For 'tis a chronicle of day by day,
Not a relation for a breakfast, nor
Befitting this first meeting. Welcome, sir,   165
This cell's my court, here have I few attendants,
And subjects none abroad; pray you, look in.
My dukedom since you have given me again,
I will requite you with as good a thing;
At least bring forth a wonder, to content ye   170
As much as me my dukedom.

[*Here* PROSPERO *discovers* FERDINAND *and* MIRANDA
playing at chess]

Miranda
Sweet lord, you play me false.

Ferdinand
                                      No, my dearest love,
I would not for the world.

Miranda
Yes, for a score of kingdoms you should wrangle,
And I would call it fair play.

173

176. *vision* illusion (i.e. which will disappear like the banquet in Act III, Scene iii).

177. *A . . . miracle* i.e. a supreme example of miraculous power (raising Ferdinand from the dead). Sebastian's astonishment seems greater than his resentment at Ferdinand's reappearance.
178. *threaten* look threatening.

180. *compass* enfold, encircle (perhaps indicating that Alonso is embracing his son, who is kneeling before him after coming forward from the cell).
181. *O, wonder!* it is Miranda's turn to express wonder and, herself a revelation to the courtiers, to marvel at this revelation of a new world.
182–4. *How many . . . in't* Miranda's words are unintentionally ironical if (as they seem to be) Sebastian and Antonio are unregenerate. If they *have* changed their natures, then it really is a fine *(brave)* new world, though in her present starry-eyed state it is *brave* anyway.
184. *'Tis new to thee* Prospero is only being lightly ironical. He knows that the world is less *brave* than Miranda thinks (a bad old world, in fact), but there is a loving gentleness towards her wonder in his words, too.
186. *Your . . . hours* you cannot have been acquainted for more than three hours.
186. *three hours* compare lines 136 and 223.
188–9. *Is she . . . together?* Alonso's reaction to Miranda as *maid* and *goddess* is the same as his son's (compare Act I, Scene ii, lines 421 and 427). It is possible to interpret his words as a general truth: his son has been *sever'd* from him by a girl. In marrying her Ferdinand must leave his father to become 'one flesh' with his wife (i.e. the opposite of being severed), but the girl, as daughter-in-law, will be the means of reconciling father and son, perhaps more deeply uniting them than before.
188–9. *mortal . . . immortal* i.e. Miranda is a mortal maid. Providence the immortal goddess.
191. *advice* considered opinion (and presumably his backing).
193. *Of whom . . . renown* of whose high reputation I have heard so often.

Alonso
                                   If this prove   175
    A vision of the island, one dear son
    Shall I twice lose.
Sebastian
                        A most high miracle!
Ferdinand
    Though the seas threaten, they are merciful;
    I have curs'd them without cause.

                        [Kneels]

Alonso
                                   Now all the blessings
    Of a glad father compass thee about!   180
    Arise, and say how thou cam'st here.
Miranda
                                   O, wonder!
    How many goodly creatures are there here!
    How beauteous mankind is! O brave new world
    That has such people in't!
Prospero
                        'Tis new to thee.
Alonso
    What is this maid with whom thou wast at play?   185
    Your eld'st acquaintance cannot be three hours,
    Is she the goddess that hath sever'd us,
    And brought us thus together?
Ferdinand
                        Sir, she is mortal;
    But by immortal Providence she's mine.
    I chose her when I could not ask my father   190
    For his advice, nor thought I had one. She
    Is daughter to this famous Duke of Milan,
    Of whom so often I have heard renown
    But never saw before; of whom I have
    Receiv'd a second life, and second father   195
    This lady makes him to me.

196. *I am hers* I am (now) her father (in that Prospero is now yours).

198. *my child* i.e. Miranda (now his child, whose forgiveness he must ask for wronging her father).

200. *heaviness* sorrow (compare *heaviness may endure for a night, hut joy cometh in the morning. Psalms, XXX. 5*).

200. *inly wept* i.e. Gonzalo's heart has been too full (with tears of joy) for him to speak. (Perhaps he feels that he should, as part of his job and in civilized behaviour, *have spoke ere this,* and needs to offer an explanation of his uncharacteristic speechlessness.)

202. *crown* a single crown, uniting Naples and Milan. ('Holy Gonzalo', loyal to Naples and Milan, is suitably the central priest-figure at this point.)

203. *chalk'd forth* marked out (with chalk-marks at points along the road?). Shakespeare's only other use of 'chalk' as a verb is in *Henry VIII*, Act I, Scene i, line 60: *whose grace chalks successors their way.*

204. *Amen* so be it. Alonso assents to Gonzalo's prayer.

205–6. *Milan . . . Naples?* Prospero turned out of his dukedom in order that (to ensure that) his descendants should become Kings of Naples?

207. *common* ordinary, commonplace.

207. *set it down* inscribe it.

208. *lasting* perhaps with a suggestion of 'everlasting'.

208. *one* a single.

209. *find* meet (in the sense of 'finding a husband'?), or perhaps 'found him waiting'.

211. *Prospero his dukedom* i.e. found his dukedom.

212. *and all of us ourselves* i.e. found ourselves (the truth about ourselves).

213. *own* i.e. himself (in control of himself).

205–13. Gonzalo's speech summarizes the story of the main events with impressive economy. It is in a sense 'the last word' and all that remains is for the characters to come down to earth again with the arrival of the comic characters. Boatswain and comic trio.

213. *Give me your hands* Alonso echoes Prospero's action of Act IV, Scene i.

214–15. *Let . . . joy* may grief and sorrow for ever possess (grip) the heart of anyone who does not join me in wishing you every happiness. (Prospero has embraced Alonso, and then Gonzalo; Alonso has embraced Ferdinand, and perhaps Miranda. Their embracing has been a loving and happy action. The only embracing received by the hard-hearted, e.g. Sebastian and Antonio, is given by unhappiness.)

Stage Direction, *amazedly* in a bewildered state.

Alonso
                                        I am hers.
But, O, how oddly will it sound that I
Must ask my child forgiveness!
Prospero
                                        There, sir, stop;
Let us not burden our remembrances with
A heaviness that's gone.
Gonzalo
                                        I have inly wept,   200
Or should have spoke ere this. Look down, you
    gods,
And on this couple drop a blessed crown;
For it is you that have chalk'd forth the way
Which brought us hither.
Alonso
                                        I say. Amen, Gonzalo!

Gonzalo
Was Milan thrust from Milan, that his issue   205
Should become Kings of Naples? O, rejoice
Beyond a common joy, and set it down
With gold on lasting pillars: in one voyage
Did Claribel her husband find at Tunis;
And Ferdinand, her brother, found a wife   210
Where he himself was lost; Prospero his dukedom
In a poor isle; and all of us ourselves
When no man was his own.
Alonso
[To FERDINAND and MIRANDA]   Give me your hands.
Let grief and sorrow still embrace his heart
That doth not wish you joy.
Gonzalo
                                        Be it so. Amen!   215

*[Re-enter ARIEL, with the master and boatswain
amazedly following]*

O look, sir, look, sir! Here is more of us!
I prophesied, if a gallows were on land,

218. *blasphemy* you blasphemous fellow.

219. *swear'st grace o'erboard* i.e. by swearing, removes God's grace (divine protection) from the ship.

221. *best news* i.e. that we are talking with you now.

223. *Which . . . spilt* which only three hours ago we said had gone on the rocks (was wrecked).

224. *tight and yare* ship-shape, trim and ready.

226. *tricksy* ingenious, clever.

227–8. *strengthen . . . stranger* grow stranger and stranger (to listen to).

230. *of sleep* asleep. (The resurrection image is reinforced by *dead:* the mariners have also been roused and raised from a metaphorical death.)

231. *clapp'd under hatches* i.e. imprisoned below deck (compare the phrase 'clapped in irons').

232. *but even now* only a moment ago.

232. *several* separate, distinct. (Compare Act III, Scene i, line 42.)

235. *We were awak'd* i.e. we were woken up by the *strange and several noises.* The inverted construction puts the actions in their right sequence: first, the noises, then the waking up. (The noises seem to be those of prisoners in chains: the mariners have not been in irons, but their release from below the hatches would seem as if they had been.)

236. *in all her trim* compare *tight and yare* in line 224. The ship was spick and span, and ready to sail. (Like the garments of the nobles, the vessel seems fresher than before.)

236. *Freshly* once more, afresh (though there is also the sense of the ship being beheld freshly rigged out).

237. *royal . . . gallant* i.e. royal (because carrying the king), good (because sound), and gallant (because fine, 'brave'). 'Royal' and 'gallant' are also used to describe certain masts and sails: the Boatswain is not simply describing the ship's qualities but also her appearance.

237–8. *our master . . . her* 'Our Captain jumping for joy at seeing her (in such good shape).' The Master would no doubt have been confined to his cabin and so separated from his crew as suited his position, otherwise he would presumably have told the story. (Also his part being one for a minor actor in Act I, Scene i, and the Boatswain's for an actor of some power, the Master would be less suitable to give the graphic account, and in fact is given nothing to say!)

238. *On a trice* in a flash, suddenly.

239. *we* i.e. Master and Boatswain.

239. *them* i.e. the ship's crew.

240. *moping* in befuddled, bewildered fashion (with suggestions of suikiness and being downcast).

241. *Bravely my diligence* splendidly, my punctilious and efficient one.

This fellow could not drown. Now, blasphemy,
That swear'st grace o'erboard, not an oath on shore?
Hast thou no mouth by land? What is the news?   220

Boatswain
The best news is that we have safely found
Our King and company, the next, our ship –
Which but three glasses since we gave out split –
Is tight and yare, and bravely rigg'd, as when
We first put out to sea.

Ariel
[Aside to PROSPERO.]   Sir, all this service   225
Have I done since I went.

Prospero
[Aside to ARIEL]   My tricksy spirit!

Alonso
These are not natural events; they strengthen
From strange to stranger. Say, how came you hither?

Boatswain
If I did think, sir, I were well awake,
I'd strive to tell you. We were dead of sleep,   230
And – how, we know not – all clapp'd under hatches;
Where, but even now, with strange and several noises
Of roaring, shrieking, howling, jingling chains,
And more diversity of sounds, all horrible,
We were awak'd; straightway at liberty;   235
Where we, in all her trim, freshly beheld
Our royal, good, and gallant ship; our master
Cap'ring to eye her. On a trice, so please you,
Even in a dream, were we divided from them,
And were brought moping hither.

Ariel
[Aside to PROSPERO]   Was't well done?   240

Prospero
[Aside to ARIEL] Bravely, my diligence. Thou shalt be
    free.

242. *maze . . . trod* see note to Act III, Scene iii, line 2. The image is that of trying to reach the truth along the tortuous paths of life's labyrinthine journey with its unexpected and baffling twists and turns.

244. *conduct* conductor, guide.

245. *my liege* although Alonso has resigned Milan to Prospero (line 118), as a king he is still senior to him and is therefore courteously addressed as *liege*, sovereign lord.

246. *infest* trouble, agitate.

246. *beating on* 'hammering away at (in your mind).' Compare Act I, Scene ii, line 176 and Act IV, Scene i, line 162. (And also compare *King Lear,* Act III, Scene iv, line 14: *The tempest in my mind Doth from my senses take all feeling else Save what beats there.)*

247–50. *at pick'd . . . accidents* at a suitable opportunity in the near future, I'll give you an explanation in private, and show it to be perfectly capable of proof, of each of the events which have just taken place.

251. *well* as being for the best.

253. *How . . . sir?* how are you getting on, my noble lord? Alonso is still bemused, and Prospero speaks to him as a doctor might to a patient 'coming round'.

255. *odd* extra.

256–7. *Every . . . fortune* perhaps Stephano is trying to show leadership by saying that they must all work together in spite of any setbacks, though it sounds more as though he has unwittingly muddled his sentences and intended to say, 'Every man shift for himself . . .'.

257–8. *Coragio, bully-monster* cheer up, my fine monster, take heart.

259. *true spies* truthful eyes, (literally, spies who bring an accurate report of what they have seen).

261. *O Setebos* Caliban swears by his *clam's god* (see Act I, Scene ii, line 373).

261. *brave spirits* Caliban's exclamation echoes Miranda's in line 182.

262. *How fine my master is* i.e. dressed as Duke of Milan.

Alonso

    This is as strange a maze as e'er men trod;
    And there is in this business more than nature
    Was ever conduct of. Some oracle
    Must rectify our knowledge.

Prospero

                  Sir, my liege,   245
    Do not infest your mind with beating on
    The strangeness of this business; at pick'd leisure,
    Which shall be shortly, single I'll resolve you,
    Which to you shall seem probable, of every
    These happen'd accidents; till when, be cheerful   250
    And think of each thing well. *[Aside to* ARIEL*]* Come
        hither, spirit;
    Set Caliban and his companions free;
    Untie the spell.

              [Exit ARIEL*]*

              How fares my gracious sir?
    There are yet missing of your company
    Some few odd lads that you remember not.   255

    [Re-enter ARIEL, *driving in* CALIBAN, STEPHANO, *and*
        TRINCULO, *in their stolen apparel]*

Stephano

    Every man shift for all the rest, and let no man take
    care for himself; for all is but fortune. Coragio, bully-
    monster, coragio!

Trinculo

    If these be true spies which I wear in my head, here's
    a goodly sight.   260

Caliban

    O Setebos, these be brave spirits indeed!
    How fine my master is! I am afraid
    He will chastise me.

265–6. Will . . . marketable Sebastian and Antonio treat Caliban (and less seriously, Stephano and Trinculo) as mere things from which to make a profit at a fair, and thus precisely parallel Stephano and Trinculo's first reactions to Caliban.

265–6. plain fish clearly a fish (presumably from the smell: see note to Act II, Scene ii, line 26).

267. Mark but the badges just look at the livery coat-of-arms. Prospero is either drawing attention to the royal arms of Naples on Stephano's and Trinculo's own clothing or to the ducal arms of Milan on their stolen garments. In either case they are not *true* (i.e. honest) men because they are wearing stolen garments. (There could also be an implicit reference to Antonio, who metaphorically put on the livery of Naples over that of Milan.) *Badges* may, however, mean simply the stolen garments.

268. This as for this.

270. That that she.

271. dead . . . power exercise the authority of the moon but independently of the moon itself, (i.e. she received her power from her witchcraft and not from the moon).

272–3. demi-devil –/For he's a bastard i.e. neither pure devil nor purely human but the product of the Devil and a witch. See Act I, Scene ii, line 319.

275. thing of darkness (a) Caliban, born of evil, (b) Caliban, dark-skinned. (Prospero may also be referring to Caliban as the dark, animal side or part of his own nature as a human being, with Miranda and/or Ariel perhaps symbolizing his fair, spiritual side.)

279. reeling ripe staggering drunkenly (full of wine).

280. grand liquor potent brew.

280. gilded flushed their faces (i.e. they were 'all lit up').

282. pickle state, mess (a) from their soaking in the pond, (b) because drunk, (c) because caught thieving.

283. pickle Trinculo, professional jester, can still manage a weak pun: *pickle* now becomes the wine (vinegar) in which his body is saturated, steeped.

283–4. I . . . flyblowing i.e. because his body is 'meat' preserved in pickling alcohol, and flies will therefore not contaminate it (only laying their eggs in fresh or decomposing flesh).

286. Stephano, but a cramp one great cramp, aching all over.

Sebastian
             Ha, ha!
What things are these, my lord Antonio?
Will money buy 'em?

Antonio
                      Very like; one of them   265
Is a plain fish, and no doubt marketable.

Prospero
Mark but the badges of these men, my lords,
Then say if they be true. This mis-shapen knave –
His mother was a witch, and one so strong
That could control the moon, make flows and ebbs,   270
And deal in her command without her power.
These three have robb'd me; and this demi-devil –
For he's a bastard one – had plotted with them
To take my life. Two of these fellows you
Must know and own; this thing of darkness I   275
Acknowledge mine.

Caliban
               I shall be pinch'd to death.

Alonso
Is not this Stephano, my drunken butler?

Sebastian
He is drunk now; where had he wine?

Alonso
And Trinculo is reeling ripe; where should they
Find this grand liquor that hath gilded 'em?   280
How cam'st thou in this pickle?

Trinculo
I have been in such a pickle since I saw you last that,
I fear me, will never out of my bones. I shall not fear
flyblowing.

Sebastian
Why, how now, Stephano!   285

Stephano
O, touch me not; I am not Stephano, but a cramp.

Prospero
You'd be king 'o the isle, sirrah?

288. *a sore one* probably further punning, i.e. (a) aching, (b) sorry, (c) strict.

290. *disproportion'd in his manners* ugly in his behaviour.

292. *look* hope, expect.

295. *grace* pardon, mercy.
295. *thrice-double* probably of no particular significance as an epithet, but Shakespeare uses the prefix 'thrice' quite often, usually in praising. There are four instances in his plays of 'thrice-noble', and *thrice-double ass* could be the antithesis of 'thrice-noble lord'. (Perhaps *ass* because an ass carried the drunken Silenus about, who though not a god himself was foster-father to a god, Bacchus, god of wine.)
297. *worship* respect, honour, reverence.
297. *dull fool* stupid idiot, (i.e. Alonso's Fool or Jester should have been sharp-witted, whereas Trinculo has been duped).
297. *go to* that's enough, get on with it.
298. *luggage* see note to Act IV, Scene i, line 231.

300. *train* retinue, followers.

302. *waste* spend, use up.

305. *accidents* events.

307. *bring* escort, accompany, conduct.

311. *Every . . . grave* perhaps connected with Act IV, Scene i, line 3, in which case one thought is for Miranda, one for Milan, and one for his own approaching end.

Stephano
     I should have been a sore one, then.
Alonso
     [*Pointing to* CALIBAN] This is as strange a thing as e'er
          I look'd on.
Prospero
     He is as disproportion'd in his manners   290
     As in his shape. Go, sirrah, to my cell;
     Take with you your companions; as you look
     To have my pardon, trim it handsomely.
Caliban
     Ay, that I will; and I'll be wise hereafter,
     And seek for grace. What a thrice-double ass   295
     Was I to take this drunkard for a god,
     And worship this dull fool!
Prospero
                              Go to; away!
Alonso
     Hence, and bestow your luggage where you found it.
Sebastian
     Or stole it, rather.

          [*Exeunt* CALIBAN, STEPHANO, *and* TRINCULO]

Prospero
     Sir, I invite your Highness and your train   300
     To my poor cell, where you shall take your rest
     For this one night; which, part of it, I'll waste
     With such discourse as, I not doubt, shall make it
     Go quick away – the story of my life,
     And the particular accidents gone by   305
     Since I came to this isle. And in the morn
     I'll bring you to your ship, and so to Naples,
     Where I have hope to see the nuptial
     Of these our dear-belov'd solemnized,
     And thence retire me to my Milan, where   310
     Every third thought shall be my grave.

313. *Take the ear strangely* strike one as something very unusual, rare.
313. *deliver all* tell it in detail.
314. *auspicious gales* favourable (i.e. following) winds.
315–16. *And sail . . . far off* and such speedy sailing that you will soon
overtake the rest of your royal fleet, which is already well on its way.

318. *Please you, draw near* please go in (to the cell). As the actors enter
the cell, Prospero is left alone on the stage to speak his farewell to the
audience.

Alonso
                                        I long
To hear the story of your life, which must
Take the ear strangely.
Prospero
                              I'll deliver all;
And promise you calm seas, auspicious gales,
And sail so expeditious that shall catch   315
Your royal fleet far off. *[Aside to* ARIEL*]* My Ariel,
    chick,
That is thy charge. Then to the elements
Be free, and fare thou well! – Please you, draw near.

                    [Exeunt]

EPILOGUE

1. *Now . . . o'erthrown* now all my spells have been discarded.

3. *faint* weak, feeble.
4. *confin'd* kept here.

6. *got* got back.
7. *the deceiver* i.e. Antonio.
8. *bare* empty, uninhabited (Prospero gesturing towards the empty stage around him, perhaps).
9. *bands* bonds. Prospero, who has been binding and releasing throughout the play, now begs for his own freedom.
10. *with . . . hands* (a) by undoing or untying the *bands* with which he is bound, (b) releasing him by clapping their hands in applause.
11. *Gentle breath* kind remarks, favourable comments (like the *auspicious gales* of Act V, Scene i, line 314) on the play.
12. *project* purpose (compare Act V, Scene i, line 1).
13. *want* both meanings, wish or desire *and* lack or need, are present: i.e. Prospero desires Ariel and his spirits to force the audience to grant his release by magic spells, but he himself lacks spirits or magic to do so.
15. *despair* dejection, abandoning hope (compare *desperation,* suicidal thoughts, in Act I, Scene ii, line 210, and *desperate,* suicidal, in Act III, Scene iii, line 104).
16. *reliev'd* raised up again, restored.
16. *by prayer* (a) by my requests to you, or (b) by your intercessions for me.
17–18. *Which . . . faults* a plea which is so piercing that it reaches to the Mercy-seat of God the Judge and persuades Him to forgive all shortcomings and to give them a free pardon. (The playwright throws himself on the mercy of the audience, who are judging the play.)
19. *would . . . be* wish to be pardoned.
20. *indulgence* lenient attitude. (A Papal indulgence was a pardon remitting temporal punishment still due for sins whose eternal punishment has been sacramentally absolved.)

EPILOGUE

[Spoken by PROSPERO*]*

Now my charms are all o'erthrown,
And what strength I have's mine own,
Which is most faint. Now 'tis true,
I must be here confin'd by you,
Or sent to Naples. Let me not,   5
Since I have my dukedom got,
And pardon'd the deceiver, dwell
In this bare island by your spell;
But release me from my bands
With the help of your good hands.   10
Gentle breath of yours my sails
Must fill, or else my project fails,
Which was to please. Now I want
Spirits to enforce, art to enchant;
And my ending is despair   15
Unless I be reliev'd by prayer,
Which pierces so that it assaults
Mercy itself, and frees all faults.
As you from crimes would pardon'd be,
Let your indulgence set me free.   20

SUMMING UP

It was suggested in the Introduction that *The Tempest* is a play in which themes are more important than characters, and that the characters are perhaps best understood if viewed as *kinds* of people rather than as particular individuals; that the play does not, because it is so short, develop its characters 'warts and all'. Assuming this to be so, any comments on the characters should be linked closely with the themes illuminated by those characters: in no Shakespeare play are themes merely incidental to the characters or characters purely there to express themes, but in *The Tempest* there is an unusually close relationship between the two.

In Prospero, for example, most of the central ideas of the play converge. The idea of *discovery* and *self-discovery* can be seen in the events before as well as on the island: while still Duke in Milan he is an explorer in the realms of his magic art who also discovers truths about human nature when his brother usurps his title, as he does on the island later when he discovers that simple Caliban is as treacherous as sophisticated Antonio. He is an idealist who is forced' to become a realist. And in this 'becoming' he is an example of the theme of change which threads its way through the play: it is not only that he changes the lives of others, he is himself changed by the events he creates. The transformation of Prospero from someone exulting in having his enemies in his power, so that he can avenge the murderous wrongs done to him and his only child by them, to someone who becomes able to forgive them, is the principal metamorphosis in the play. The ideas that characters are tested by events is common to most plays, which are mirrors of the trials of life itself, it is more prominent in *The Tempest* because it is Prospero rather than accidental circumstances who is seen as doing the proving (for example, by testing Ferdinand) and he is himself tested crucially when he has to choose between 'virtue' or 'Vengeance' (Act V, Scene i, line 28). In choosing forgiveness rather than revenge, love rather than hate, he releases himself from bondage to the past. And here two threads lie close together. The idea of *imprisonment and release* is continually present in the play generally, and in Prospero particularly. As he shows in the agitated violence of his feelings about the events of his usurpation, which lie a long time off (Act I, Scene ii, lines 66–168), twelve years back, the past is still vividly present and real: he is still imprisoned by its memory. He spellbinds and releases characters during the play, but it is himself whom he releases in releasing them. Much of the play is about *freedom* and how Prospero and the other characters achieve it at different spiritual and physical levels. (It is rather appropriate that he should leave his *cell* at the end of the play.)

The Tempest has sometimes been criticized for lacking any true dramatic conflict, because Prospero is so powerful that he can manipulate the characters like puppets. What is often overlooked is that he cannot control their wills (boiling their brains within their skulls is equivalent to anaesthetizing them temporarily), and more important, that the conflict is within Prospero himself. He may *control* the characters physically, but it is the exercise of *self-control* that Prospero has to learn. In order to become a magician he has had to learn the art of self-discipline; it is during the play and at the most testing moment for him that he has to exercise that self-control through which he restrains himself from taking his revenge.

It is only through self-control that men can effectively or productively govern others, and Prospero shows how difficult this exercise of control is to achieve in his relationship with his two servants, Ariel and Caliban. When Ariel protests (Act I, Scene ii, lines 242–9) that Prospero has not yet released him as promised, he receives a sharp reply from his master, so anxious is Prospero not to lose him at the very moment when he is most needed. Ariel symbolizes Man's spiritual nature or his imagination, and it is possible to see Prospero as representing the artist managing the materials of his art through the control of his creative imagination. The rebellious Ariel, like the artist's imagination, is controlled and put to creative use only with difficulty, though once under control he is as joyful and rapid as the imagination working without restraint. Prospero's other servant, Caliban, is also rebellious and needs to be kept under control: *he is this thing of darkness* (Act V, Scene i, line 275) which Prospero acknowledges as his own, the animal part of human nature with its potentially destructive drives needing to be put to constructive use.

Caliban is shown as raw nature needing to be nurtured, or educated. (The play repeats the idea of educating oneself and others in a number of places.) During the play it seems that Prospero, who like all artists is a teacher, has failed to civilize him and despairs of doing so. And when Antonio and Sebastian appear to be unrepentant at the end of the play it looks as though Prospero will have to accept that there is a dark part of human personality which is incapable of reformation. Yet perhaps Caliban suggests that there is always hope even in the hardest of hard cases, when he says that he will be *wise hereafter, and seek for grace* (Act V, Scene i, lines 294–5).

Throughout the play there is a strong feeling that events are moving towards a future, and that 'hereafter' men will lead changed lives. Prospero's part is to control the present so that a fruitful future can follow. *Time* in one form or another is insistently referred to: in Prospero's looking into the past, and in his awareness of the need to seize his opportunities in the present to redeem the past and prepare the future. He can be seen as the older generation handing over hopefully to the younger. Yet though he uses Time to bring good out of evil, he recognizes that as a human being he is himself subject to

Providence divine and to a destiny which is shaping his end also.

His marriage-masque for Miranda and Ferdinand is the best gift that he can present to them, being a wise vision of life's potentiality. A sense of *wonder* is the response of the lovers to the masque, just as it is the reaction of most of the characters to the events on the island. And although it is the impresario-figure Prospero who presents these wonders, he is capable of being surprised himself (for example, when Miranda is able to recall infant memories from *the dark backward and abysm of time*) and his daughter's name may indicate his wonder at having a daughter. In fact the capacity for being surprised and able to wonder seems to belong to all the characters except the cynical Antonio and Sebastian. The origins of the theme no doubt lie in the *Sea Adventure* source (see Introduction and the Appendix) and the feeling of miraculous escape, and lead through the stage devices used in masque-theatre to the idea that truths can suddenly be revealed to men, and often under the pressure of disorientating experiences.

Prospero is not the only character who expresses the central concerns of the play: all the characters relate to them in a variety of ways, and express other themes as well. Among these themes may be found one which Shakespeare reiterates throughout his work, the idea of *loyalty and treachery*. He juxtaposes the loyalty of the selfless Gonzalo with the treachery of the self-seeking Antonio and Sebastian, and underlines their plot against Alonso in the comic sub-plot of Caliban, Trinculo and Stephano's plan to murder Prospero. The idea of playing false can be seen in Prospero's warning to Ferdinand and Miranda to be true to their vows of chastity, and even perhaps in Miranda's gentle rebuke *My lord, you play me false* (Act V, Scene i, line 172). Even Miranda is guilty of breaking her vow inadvertently when she gives her name to Ferdinand (Act III, Scene i, line 37). All instances of disloyalty reflect Antonio's initial treachery towards Prospero, which is not only that of subject to ruler in the state but of younger to older brother in the microcosm of the state, the family.

Acts of treachery are breaches of that natural, divinely-ordered hierarchical system which was for Elizabethans the basis of society. When Gonzalo describes his ideal classless commonwealth (Act II, Scene i, lines 143–59) he is expressing not only contemporary hopes of finding and founding a brave new world on the far side of the Atlantic, but is conscious that the visionary Utopia he is proposing is unlikely to replace a hierarchical society, men being what they are. The sneering cynicism of Antonio and Sebastian is exposed by their reaction to his day-dreaming; their dreams are only of personal power based upon things remaining as they are. Nevertheless, though Gonzalo is realist enough to know that his Utopia is hardly a practical possibility, he also knows that men can only live by hope of a better future. As a character he is like others in *The Tempest*, both a person and a figure. On the ship he shows the fear that any human being would, on the island he becomes the embodiment of Faith, Hope and Charity. At the mock-banquet (Act III, Scene iii,) he says that Alonso should put more trust in Providence (*Faith sir, you need not fear*); he shows a more than merely diplomatic cheerfulness in contrast to Alonso's despair; and his charitable actions are gratefully referred to by Prospero in Act I, Scene ii, lines 160–8. Whether or not Shakespeare was intending to convey a specifically Christian message in *The Tempest* is probably a matter of opinion and emphasis, but much of its terminology (words like *holy*, *grace*, *mercy*, *blessed*, *pardon*) echoes New Testament language, as do themes and images of resurrection and forgiveness.

The idea of *loss* and *recovery* is also important: through loss the characters are tested and learn. Prospero learns patience through the loss of his dukedom; Alonso learns remorse through the loss of Ferdinand; in losing something precious, something more precious is found. As well as experiencing the loss of family and friends, the characters find that they have lost their way (symbolically, in life) as they tread the maze (Act III, Scene iii, line 2) of the island's paths and find no way out. The theme is summed up in Act V, Scene i, lines 205–13 when Gonzalo says that in the moment of loss they each 'found themselves', and there is an echo in his words of the Christian message that whoever loses his life shall find it.

Shakespeare's comic scenes exist partly to provide relief from the tensions of the main action and partly to reflect the main themes. In the Trinculo-Stephano sub-plot their words and actions parody and caricature much of the serious content of the play: a distorting mirror is held up and we laugh as we see the truth. Their drunken imitation of court behaviour (Act III, Scene ii, lines 1–55), their greedy plotting to seize power by murder (Act III, Scene ii, lines 56–110), their shallow preoccupation with the trappings of authority (Act IV, Scene i, lines 222–53) precisely echo the main themes of self-control, treachery and deceit. In their scale of values a bottle becomes a Bible, and when they complain (Act IV, Scene i, lines 208–10) that there is disgrace and dishonour in its loss in the pool, we are reminded of the dignity and seriousness of the upper level of the action. The way in which the comic can recall and underline the tragic is shown when Caliban says *All's hushed as midnight yet* (Act IV, Scene i, line 207) on the threshold of Prospero's cell, and we remember that *midnight fated to the purpose* (Act I, Scene ii, lines 128–9) of twelve years before.

As a trio, Caliban, Trinculo and Stephano provide an image of the turbulence and discord which contrast with the harmony created by Prospero as he imposes order on uncontrolled nature by means of reason and the development of self-discipline: they speak a blunt prose which contrasts with the musical verse of the main plot, the rough rhythms and words of their songs are the antithesis of Ariel's sweet airs, their response to his tabor and pipe is that of *unback'd colts*, wild animals.

Music is the most important element in *The Tempest*, both as stage-sound and as symbol, it is no mere ornament. Shakespeare uses it to create an ambiance in which we accept the supernatural events; Prospero uses it as the medium through which he exercises his magic, after the realistic chaos of the storm scene, which presents a picture of actual life with its dangers and disorders, music removes the action to a higher and more abstract plane of existence so that we see the characters in their essence and as representative human beings. Ferdinand and Miranda are not so much two unique and individualized personalities as the embodiment of romantic love: they are all lovers who fall in love at first sight (and have their first tiff – Act V, Scene i, line 172), whose falling in love is a wonderful discovery, and whose only wish is to serve each other faithfully. The words of their duet in Act III, Scene i are not intended to reproduce everyday conversation but to convey the harmony of their feelings, in the way that a love-song expresses the lyrical ecstasy of emotion which is part of, but transcends, sexual passion.

Caliban's unrestrained sexual appetite is that of nature run wild. Before the masque, through which he blesses Miranda's marriage with fertility, Prospero warns Ferdinand to exercise self-control; the wanton power of Venus is thwarted and Ceres presents an image of the fruitful productiveness which results from cultivation. The device of a play-within-a-play is used on a number of occasions by Shakespeare to underline a play's main concerns by repeating them in miniature. *The Tempest* is itself a masque-like play, and Prospero's masque is a microcosm of it. The idea that the future depends upon the young – in this case Ferdinand and Miranda – to bring a brave new world into being from the bad old world of their parents is the message of the play, and when the goddesses bless the betrothal with harmony and fruitfulness they present a vision of the outcome of Prospero's plan.

If we approach *The Tempest* expecting realism in

characterization, plot or setting we will be disappointed. It is too compressed a play for more than a limited development of its characters; and the characters themselves are too restricted in independence of action to achieve their aims without Prospero's manipulation. The fact that we do not experience the events in Milan at first hand – events from which the action stems – together with references to how remote the events are in time and space, helps to set the events on the island at a distance from reality. At the same time there is a concentration of language which combines with an economy of action to produce a picture of life rather than life itself. Shakespeare was exploring beyond realism in his final Romances to create plays which have the timeless poetic power of fairy-tales and myths, yet remain part of the ordinary world of particular timebound events.

THEME INDEX

The central theme in the play is that of *metamorphosis* or *change*; many of the transformations are produced within the characters by the external action of Prospero's magic. Closely associated with change is the key word strange.

Change:
I ii 66–109 (in Antonio); Ariel's various costume changes; I ii 401–2; the sudden end of the Masque in IV; IV i 147–55; IV i 246–8; Prospero changes heart V i 20–30, and costume V i 85–6.
Prospero's magic works through music, which represents order, the sweet music of Ariel's songs, the harsh music of thunder, the stirring music of tabor and pipe. Comic songs contrast with the solemn and supernatural airs.

Music:
I ii 375–405; II i 177 (stage direction) and 291–300; II ii 41–55, 173–80; III ii 116–48; III iii 18, 82, 97–9; IV i 59, 105–16, 174–7; Vi 58, 88–94.
It is in human relationships that order and disorder, loyalty and treachery, are most fully displayed in this as in all Shakespeare's plays, on the political, social, family or personal level.

Relationships:
I i (throughout); I ii 56–9, 66–77, 118–22; Prospero with Ariel, I ii 250–300, and throughout the play; with Caliban, I ii 344–74, and throughout the play; II i 67–8, 143–59; II ii 68–78; the whole of III i; the comic dissensions in III ii; IV i 14–22; V i 20–31, 71–9, 137–52, 190–9, 209–14.
Love and forgiveness set free, hatred and revenge imprison. The idea of *bondage* and *release* is expressed throughout the play.

Bondage and Release:
I ii 185–6, 230–2, 250–96, 326, 342–3, 360–2, 461, 486–94;
II ii 181–2; III i 4–15, 41, 89; III iii 2 (the maze as prison),
88–90; IV i 120–1, 180–1, 263–5; V i 7–11, 30–2, 41–57,
58–68, 79–82, 231–6, 252–3, 319–20, Epilogue 4–10,
19–20.
Sleep is a sort of bondage yet asleep we can escape in our
dreams.

Sleep and Dreams:
I ii 45, 185–6, 486; II i 181–96, 205–12, 296–301; III ii
58–9, 83–4, 133–9; IV i 56–8;V i 48–50, 98–100, 230–5,
239. A 'brave new world' is revealed through *discovery*
and accompanied by feelings of *wonder*, *amazement*,
strangeness and *rarity*.

Discovery and Wonder:
I ii 14, 198, 306, 406–7, 409–33; II i 6–8, 192–3, 207, 314;
II ii throughout; III i 37–48; III ii 131–2; III iii 18–95; IV
i 7, 118–24; V i 104–17, 154–62, 170, 178, 181–4, 227–8,
242–4, 261–2, 313–18.
The old world of the past is redeemed by the new world
of a hopeful future. The present moment ('now') is a tense
turning-point for all the characters. References to *time* are
frequent and often related to *fate* or *destiny*.

Time and Fate:
I ii 36–41, 50, 53, 128–9, 159, 178–84, 228, 239–40, 279,
296, 298; II i 12, 175–7, 241–5, III i 22, 40, 95; III iii 53,
68–75, 104–6; IV i 141–2,144–5, 246, 261–5; V i 1–5, 93,
101, 136, 186, 223, 302.
Prospero is the subject and the agent of destiny, both
man and superman. He is grappling with problems which
exist in himself as well as in others. His magical powers,
like those of an artist (playwright, poet, painter or musi-
cian), create (or release) an ideal world from the real one.

Magic:
I ii 1, 24–5, 185–6, 291, 372, 467–74; II i 59–61; III ii 87–91; III iii 17, 52, 82, 88; IV i 35–41, 60–137, 257–60; V i 50–7.

Sea:
I i 16, 56–9; I ii 1–5, 145–58, 170, 175–7, 210–11, 233–5, 252–3, 301, 375–405, 435–7, 462; II i 59–62, 107–18, 215–23, 232–3, 245–6, II ii 25–7, 42–3, 116–31; III ii 11–14; III iii 8–10, 55–6, 63–4, 71–5, 100–2, IV i 69–70; V i 34–6, 43, 56–7, 79–82, 151–2, 178, 218–25, 270, 314–16.
The sound of the sea which surrounds the island beats through the play. We are constantly reminded of its presence.

Shakespeare: Words and Phrases

adapted from the Collins English Dictionary

abate 1 VERB to abate here means to lessen or diminish ❑ *There lives within the very flame of love/A kind of wick or snuff that will abate it* (*Hamlet 4.7*) 2 VERB to abate here means to shorten ❑ *Abate thy hours* (*A Midsummer Night's Dream 3.2*) 3 VERB to abate here means to deprive ❑ *She hath abated me of half my train* (*King Lear 2.4*)

abjure VERB to abjure means to renounce or give up ❑ *this rough magic I here abjure* (*Tempest 5.1*)

abroad ADV abroad means elsewhere or everywhere ❑ *You have heard of the news abroad* (*King Lear 2.1*)

abrogate VERB to abrogate means to put an end to ❑ *so it shall praise you to abrogate scurrility* (*Love's Labours Lost 4.2*)

abuse 1 NOUN abuse in this context means deception or fraud ❑ *What should this mean? Are all the rest come back?/Or is it some abuse, and no such thing?* (*Hamlet 4.7*) 2 NOUN an abuse in this context means insult or offence ❑ *I will be deaf to pleading and excuses/Nor tears nor prayers shall purchase our abuses* (*Romeo and Juliet 3.1*) 3 NOUN an abuse in this context means using something improperly ❑ *we'll digest/Th'abuse*

of distance (*Henry II Chorus*) 4 NOUN an abuse in this context means doing something which is corrupt or dishonest ❑ *Come, bring them away: if these be good people in a commonweal that do nothing but their abuses in common houses, I know no law: bring them away.* (*Measure for Measure 2.1*)

abuser NOUN the abuser here is someone who betrays, a betrayer ❑ *I ... do attach thee/For an abuser of the world* (*Othello 1.2*)

accent NOUN accent here means language ❑ *In states unborn, and accents yet unknown* (*Julius Caesar 3.1*)

accident NOUN an accident in this context is an event or something that happened ❑ *think no more of this night's accidents* (*A Midsummer Night's Dream 4.1*)

accommodate VERB to accommodate in this context means to equip or to give someone the equipment to do something ❑ *The safer sense will ne'er accommodate/His master thus.* (*King Lear 4.6*)

according ADJ according means sympathetic or ready to agree ❑ *within the scope of choice/Lies*

my consent and fair according voice
(*Romeo and Juliet* 1.2)

account NOUN account often means
judgement (by God) or reckoning
❑ *No reckoning made, but sent to my
account/ With all my imperfections on
my head* (*Hamlet* 1.5)

accountant ADJ accountant here
means answerable or accountable
❑ *his offence is… /Accountant to the
law* (*Measure for Measure* 2.4)

ace NOUN ace here means one or first
referring to the lowest score on a dice
❑ *No die, but an ace, for him; for he is
but one./ Less than an ace, man; for he
is dead; he is nothing.* (*A Midsummer
Night's Dream* 5.1)

acquit VERB here acquit means to be
rid of or free of. It is related to the
verb quit ❑ *I am glad I am so acquit
of this tinderbox* (*The Merry Wives of
Windsor* 1.3)

afeard ADJ afeard means afraid or
frightened ❑ *Nothing afeard of what
thyself didst make* (*Macbeth* 1.3)

affiance NOUN affiance means
confidence or trust ❑ *O how hast
thou with jealousy infected/ The
sweetness of affiance* (*Henry V* 2.2)

affinity NOUN in this context, affinity
means important connections, or
relationships with important people
❑ *The Moor replies/ That he you hurt
is of great fame in Cyprus,/ And great
affinity* (*Othello* 3.1)

agnize VERB to agnize is an old
word that means that you recognize
or acknowledge something ❑ *I do
agnize/ A natural and prompt alacrity
I find in hardness* (*Othello* 1.3)

ague NOUN an ague is a fever in
which the patient has hot and cold

shivers one after the other ❑ *This
is some monster of the isle with four
legs, who hath got … an ague* (*The
Tempest* 2.2)

alarm, alarum NOUN an alarm or
alarum is a call to arms or a signal for
soldiers to prepare to fight ❑ *Whence
cometh this alarum and the noise?*
(*Henry VI part I* 1.4)

Albion NOUN Albion is another
word for England ❑ *but I will sell my
dukedom,/ To buy a slobbery and a
dirty farm In that nook-shotten isle of
Albion* (*Henry V* 3.5)

all of all PHRASE all of all means
everything, or the sum of all things
❑ *The very all of all* (*Love's Labours
Lost* 5.1)

amend VERB amend in this context
means to get better or to heal ❑ *at
his touch… They presently amend*
(*Macbeth* 4.3)

anchor VERB if you anchor on
something you concentrate on it or
fix on it ❑ *My invention … Anchors
on Isabel* (*Measure for Measure* 2.4)

anon ADV anon was a common word
for soon ❑ *You shall see anon how the
murderer gets the love of Gonzago's
wife* (*Hamlet* 3.2)

antic 1 ADJ antic here means weird
or strange ❑ *I'll charm the air to give
a sound/ While you perform your antic
round* (*Macbeth* 4.1) 2 NOUN in
this context antic means a clown or
a strange, unattractive creature ❑ *If
black, why nature, drawing an antic,/
Made a foul blot* (*Much Ado About
Nothing* 3.1)

apace ADV apace was a common word
for quickly ❑ *Come apace* (*As You
Like It* 3.3)

apparel NOUN apparel means clothes or clothing ❏ *one suit of apparel* (*Hamlet 3.2*)

appliance NOUN appliance here means cure ❏ *Diseases desperate grown/By desperate appliance are relieved* (*Hamlet 4.3*)

argument NOUN argument here means a topic of conversation or the subject ❏ *Why 'tis the rarest argument of wonder that hath shot out in our latter times* (*All's Well That Ends Well 2.3*)

arrant ADJ arrant means absolute, complete. It strengthens the meaning of a noun ❏ *Fortune, that arrant whore* (*King Lear 2.4*)

arras NOUN an arras is a tapestry, a large cloth with a picture sewn on it using coloured thread ❏ *Behind the arras I'll convey myself/To hear the process* (*Hamlet 3.3*)

art 1 NOUN art in this context means knowledge ❏ *Their malady convinces/The great essay of art* (*Macbeth 4.3*) 2 NOUN art can also mean skill as it does here ❏ *He ... gave you such a masterly report/For art and exercise in your defence* (*Hamlet 4.7*) 3 NOUN art here means magic ❏ *Now I want/Spirits to enforce, art to enchant* (*The Tempest 5 Epilogue*)

assay 1 NOUN an assay was an attempt, a try ❏ *Make assay./Bow, stubborn knees* (*Hamlet 3.3*) 2 NOUN assay can also mean a test or a trial ❏ *he hath made assay of her virtue* (*Measure for Measure 3.1*)

attend (on/upon) VERB attend on means to wait for or to expect ❏ *Tarry I here, I but attend on death* (*Two Gentlemen of Verona 3.1*)

auditor NOUN an auditor was a member of an audience or someone who listens ❏ *I'll be an auditor* (*A Midsummer Night's Dream 3.1*)

aught NOUN aught was a common word which meant anything ❏ *if my love thou holdest at aught* (*Hamlet 4.3*)

aunt 1 NOUN an aunt was another word for an old woman and also means someone who talks a lot or a gossip ❏ *The wisest aunt telling the saddest tale* (*A Midsummer Night's Dream 2.1*) 2 NOUN aunt could also mean a mistress or a prostitute ❏ *the thrush and the jay/Are summer songs for me and my aunts/While we lie tumbling in the hay* (*The Winter's Tale 4.3*)

avaunt EXCLAM avaunt was a common word which meant go away ❏ *Avaunt, you curs!* (*King Lear 3.6*)

aye ADV here aye means always or ever ❏ *Whose state and honour I for aye allow* (*Richard II 5.2*)

baffle VERB baffle meant to be disgraced in public or humiliated ❏ *I am disgraced, impeached, and baffled here* (*Richard II 1.1*)

bald ADJ bald means trivial or silly ❏ *I knew 'twould be a bald conclusion* (*The Comedy of Errors 2.2*)

ban NOUN a ban was a curse or an evil spell ❏ *Sometimes with lunatic bans... Enforce their charity* (*King Lear 2.3*)

barren ADJ barren meant empty or hollow ❏ *now I let go your hand, I am barren.* (*Twelfth Night 1.3*)

base ADJ base is an adjective that means unworthy or dishonourable ❏ *civet is of a baser birth than tar* (*As You Like It 3.2*)

base 1 ADJ base can also mean of low social standing or someone who was not part of the ruling class ❑ *Why brand they us with 'base'?* (*King Lear 1.2*) 2 ADJ here base means poor quality ❑ *Base cousin,/ Darest thou break first?* (*Two Noble Kinsmen 3.3*)

bawdy NOUN bawdy means obscene or rude ❑ *Bloody, bawdy villain!* (*Hamlet 2.2*)

bear in hand PHRASE bear in hand means taken advantage of or fooled ❑ *This I made good to you In our last conference, passed in probation with you/How you were borne in hand* (*Macbeth 3.1*)

beard VERB to beard someone was to oppose or confront them ❑ *Com'st thou to beard me in Denmark?* (*Hamlet 2.2*)

beard, in one's PHRASE if you say something in someone's beard you say it to their face ❑ *I will verify as much in his beard* (*Henry V 3.2*)

beaver NOUN a beaver was a visor on a battle helmet ❑ *O yes, my lord, he wore his beaver up* (*Hamlet 1.2*)

become VERB if something becomes you it suits you or is appropriate to you ❑ *Nothing in his life became him like the leaving it* (*Macbeth 1.4*)

bed, brought to PHRASE to be brought to bed means to give birth ❑ *His wife but yesternight was brought to bed* (*Titus Andronicus 4.2*)

bedabbled ADJ if something is bedabbled it is sprinkled ❑ *Bedabbled with the dew, and torn with briers* (*A Midsummer Night's Dream 3.2*)

Bedlam NOUN Bedlam was a word used for Bethlehem Hospital which was a place the insane were sent to ❑ *The country give me proof and precedent/Of Bedlam beggars* (*King Lear 2.3*)

bed-swerver NOUN a bed-swerver was someone who was unfaithful in marriage, an adulterer ❑ *she's/A bed-swerver* (*Winter's Tale 2.1*)

befall 1 VERB to befall is to happen, occur or take place ❑ *In this same interlude it doth befall/That I present a wall* (*A Midsummer Night's Dream 5.1*) 2 VERB to befall can also mean to happen to someone or something ❑ *fair befall thee and thy noble house* (*Richard III 1.3*)

behoof NOUN behoof was an advantage or benefit ❑ *All our surgeons/Convent in their behoof* (*Two Noble Kinsmen 1.4*)

beldam NOUN a beldam was a witch or old woman ❑ *Have I not reason, beldams as you are?* (*Macbeth 3.5*)

belike ADV belike meant probably, perhaps or presumably ❑ *belike he likes it not* (*Hamlet 3.2*)

bent 1 NOUN bent means a preference or a direction ❑ *Let me work,/For I can give his humour true bent,/And I will bring him to the Capitol* (*Julius Caesar 2.1*) 2 ADJ if you are bent on something you are determined to do it ❑ *for now I am bent to know/By the worst means the worst.* (*Macbeth 3.4*)

beshrew VERB beshrew meant to curse or wish evil on someone ❑ *much beshrew my manners and my pride/If Hermia meant to say Lysander lied* (*A Midsummer Night's Dream 2.2*)

betime (s) ADV betime means early ❏ *To business that we love we rise betime* (Antony and Cleopatra 4.4)

bevy NOUN bevy meant type or sort, it was also used to mean company ❏ *many more of the same bevy* (Hamlet 5.2)

blazon VERB to blazon something meant to display or show it ❏ *that thy skill be more to blazon it* (Romeo and Juliet 2.6)

blind ADJ if you are blind when you do something you are reckless or do not care about the consequences ❏ *are you yet to your own souls so blind/ That two you will war with God by murdering me* (Richard III 1.4)

bombast NOUN bombast was wool stuffing (used in a cushion for example) and so it came to mean padded out or long-winded. Here it means someone who talks a lot about nothing in particular ❏ *How now my sweet creature of bombast* (Henry IV part I 2.4)

bond 1 NOUN a bond is a contract or legal deed ❏ *Well, then, your bond, and let me see* (Merchant of Venice 1.3) 2 NOUN bond could also mean duty or commitment ❏ *I love your majesty/ According to my bond* (King Lear 1.1)

bottom NOUN here bottom means essence, main point or intent ❏ *Now I see/ The bottom of your purpose* (All's Well That Ends Well 3.7)

bounteously ADV bounteously means plentifully, abundantly ❏ *I prithee, and I'll pay thee bounteously* (Twelfth Night 1.2)

brace 1 NOUN a brace is a couple or two ❏ *Have lost a brace of kinsmen* (Romeo and Juliet 5.3) 2 NOUN if you are in a brace position it means you are ready ❏ *For that it stands not in such warlike brace* (Othello 1.3)

brand VERB to mark permanantly like the markings on cattle ❏ *the wheeled seat/ Of fortunate Caesar ... branded his baseness that ensued* (Anthony and Cleopatra 4.14)

brave ADJ brave meant fine, excellent or splendid ❏ *O brave new world/ That has such people in't* (The Tempest 5.1)

brine NOUN brine is sea-water ❏ *He shall drink nought brine, for I'll not show him/ Where the quick freshes are* (The Tempest 3.2)

brow NOUN brow in this context means appearance ❏ *doth hourly grow/ Out of his brows* (Hamlet 3.3)

burden 1 NOUN the burden here is a chorus ❏ *I would sing my song without a burden* (As You Like It 3.2) 2 NOUN burden means load or weight (this is the current meaning) ❏ *the scarfs and the bannerets about thee did manifoldly dissuade me from believing thee a vessel of too great a burden* (All's Well that Ends Well 2.3)

buttons, in one's PHRASE this is a phrase that means clear, easy to see ❏ *Tis in his buttons he will carry't* (The Merry Wives of Windsor 3.2)

cable NOUN cable here means scope or reach ❏ *The law ... Will give her cable* (Othello 1.2)

cadent ADJ if something is cadent it is falling or dropping ❏ *With cadent tears fret channels in her cheeks* (King Lear 1.4)

canker VERB to canker is to decay, become corrupt ❑ *And, as with age his body uglier grows,/ So his mind cankers* (The Tempest 4.1)

canon, from the PHRASE from the canon is an expression meaning out of order, improper ❑ *Twas from the canon* (Coriolanus 3.1)

cap-a-pie ADV cap-a-pie means from head to foot, completely ❑ *I am courtier cap-a-pie* (The Winter's Tale 4.4)

carbonadoed ADJ if something is carbonadoed it is cut or scored (scratched) with a knife ❑ *it is your carbonadoed* (All's Well That Ends Well 4.5)

carouse VERB to carouse is to drink at length, party ❑ *They cast their caps up and carouse together* (Anthony and Cleopatra 4.12)

carrack NOUN a carrack was a large old ship, a galleon ❑ *Faith, he tonight hath boarded a land-carrack* (Othello 1.2)

cassock NOUN a cassock here means a military cloak, long coat ❑ *half of the which dare not shake the snow from off their cassocks lest they shake themselves to pieces* (All's Well That Ends Well 4.3)

catastrophe NOUN catastrophe here means conclusion or end ❑ *pat he comes, like the catastrophe of the old comedy* (King Lear 1.2)

cautel NOUN a cautel was a trick or a deceptive act ❑ *Perhaps he loves you now/ And now no soil not cautel doth besmirch* (Hamlet 1.2)

celerity NOUN celerity was a common word for speed, swiftness ❑ *Hence hath offence his quick celerity/ When it is borne in high authority* (Measure for Measure 4.2)

chafe NOUN chafe meant anger or temper ❑ *this Herculean Roman does become/ The carriage of his chafe* (Anthony and Cleopatra 1.3)

chanson NOUN chanson was an old word for a song ❑ *The first row of the pious chanson will show you more* (Hamlet 2.2)

chapman NOUN a chapman was a trader or merchant ❑ *Not uttered by base sale of chapman's tongues* (Love's Labours Lost 2.1)

chaps, chops NOUN chaps (and chops) was a word for jaws ❑ *Which ne'er shook hands nor bade farewell to him/ Till he unseamed him from the nave to th' chops* (Macbeth 1.2)

chattels NOUN chattels were your moveable possessions. The word is used in the traditional marriage ceremony ❑ *She is my goods, my chattels* (The Taming of the Shrew 3.3)

chide VERB if you are chided by someone you are told off or reprimanded ❑ *Now I but chide, but I should use thee worse* (A Midsummer Night's Dream 3.2)

chinks NOUN chinks was a word for cash or money ❑ *he that can lay hold of her/ Shall have the chinks* (Romeo and Juliet 1.5)

choleric ADJ if something was called choleric it meant that they were quick to get angry ❑ *therewithal unruly waywardness that infirm and choleric years bring with them* (King Lear 1.1)

chuff NOUN a chuff was a miser,

someone who clings to his or her money ❏ *ye fat chuffs* (*Henry IV part I 2.2*)

cipher NOUN cipher here means nothing ❏ *Mine were the very cipher of a function* (*Measure for Measure 2.2*)

circummured ADJ circummured means that something is surrounded with a wall ❏ *He hath a garden circummured with brick* (*Measure for Measure 4.1*)

civet NOUN a civet is a type of scent or perfume ❏ *Give me an ounce of civet* (*King Lear 4.6*)

clamorous ADJ clamorous means noisy or boisterous ❏ *Be clamorous and leap all civil bounds* (*Twelfth Night 1.4*)

clangour, clangor NOUN clangour is a word that means ringing (the sound that bells make) ❏ *Like to a dismal clangour heard from far* (*Henry VI part III 2.3*)

cleave VERB if you cleave to something you stick to it or are faithful to it ❏ *Thy thoughts I cleave to* (*The Tempest 4.1*)

clock and clock, 'twixt PHRASE from hour to hour, without stopping or continuously ❏ *To weep 'twixt clock and clock* (*Cymbeline 3.4*)

close ADJ here close means hidden ❏ *Stand close; this is the same Athenian* (*A Midsummer Night's Dream 3.2*)

cloud NOUN a cloud on your face means that you have a troubled, unhappy expression ❏ *He has cloud in's face* (*Anthony and Cleopatra 3.2*)

cloy VERB if you cloy an appetite you satisfy it ❏ *Other women cloy/The appetites they feed* (*Anthony and Cleopatra 2.2*)

cock-a-hoop, set PHRASE if you set cock-a-hoop you become free of everything ❏ *You will set cock-a-hoop* (*Romeo and Juliet 1.5*)

colours NOUN colours is a word used to describe battle-flags or banners. Sometimes we still say that we nail our colours to the mast if we are stating which team or side of an argument we support ❏ *the approbation of those that weep this lamentable divorce under her colours* (*Cymbeline 1.5*)

combustion NOUN combustion was a word meaning disorder or chaos ❏ *prophesying ... Of dire combustion and confused events* (*Macbeth 2.3*)

comely ADJ if you are or something is comely you or it is lovely, beautiful, graceful ❏ *O, what a world is this, when what is comely/Envenoms him that bears it!* (*As You Like It 2.3*)

commend VERB if you commend yourself to someone you send greetings to them ❏ *Commend me to my brother* (*Measure for Measure 1.4*)

compact NOUN a compact is an agreement or a contract ❏ *what compact mean you to have with us?* (*Julius Caesar 3.1*)

compass 1 NOUN here compass means range or scope ❏ *you would sound me from my lowest note to the top of my compass* (*Hamlet 3.2*) 2 VERB to compass here means to achieve, bring about or make happen ❏ *How now shall this be compassed?/Canst thou bring me to the party?* (*Tempest 3.2*)

comptible ADJ comptible is an old word meaning sensitive ❏ *I am very comptible, even to the least sinister usage.* (Twelfth Night 1.5)

confederacy NOUN a confederacy is a group of people usually joined together to commit a crime. It is another word for a conspiracy ❏ *Lo, she is one of this confederacy!* (A Midsummer Night's Dream 3.2)

confound VERB if you confound something you confuse it or mix it up; it also means to stop or prevent ❏ *A million fail, confounding oath on oath.* (A Midsummer Night's Dream 3.2)

contagion NOUN contagion is an old word for disease or poison ❏ *hell itself breathes out/ Contagion to this world* (Hamlet 3.2)

contumely NOUN contumely is an old word for an insult ❏ *the proud man's contumely* (Hamlet 3.1)

counterfeit 1 VERB if you counterfeit something you copy or imitate it ❏ *Meantime your cheeks do counterfeit our roses* (Henry VI part I 2.4) 2 VERB in this context counterfeit means to pretend or make believe ❏ *I will counterfeit the bewitchment of some popular man* (Coriolanus)

coz NOUN coz was a shortened form of the word cousin ❏ *sweet my coz, be merry* (As You Like It 1.2)

cozenage NOUN cozenage is an old word meaning cheating or a deception ❏ *Thrown out his angle for my proper life,/ And with such coz'nage* (Hamlet 5.2)

crave VERB crave used to mean to beg or request ❏ *I crave your pardon* (The Comedy of Errors 1.2)

crotchet NOUN crotchets are strange ideas or whims ❏ *thou hast some strange crotchets in thy head now* (The Merry Wives of Windsor 2.1)

cuckold NOUN a cuckold is a man whose wife has been unfaithful to him ❏ *As there is no true cuckold but calamity* (Twelfth Night 1.5)

cuffs, go to PHRASE this phrase meant to fight ❏ *the player went to cuffs in the question* (Hamlet 2.2)

cup VERB in this context cup is a verb which means to pour drink or fill glasses with alcohol ❏ *cup us til the world go round* (Anthony and Cleopatra 2.7)

cur NOUN cur is an insult meaning dog and is also used to mean coward ❏ *Out, dog! out, cur! Thou drivest me past the bounds/ Of maiden's patience* (A Midsummer Night's Dream 3.2)

curiously ADV in this context curiously means carefully or skilfully ❏ *The sleeves curiously cut* (The Taming of the Shrew 4.3)

curry VERB curry means to flatter or to praise someone more than they are worth ❏ *I would curry with Master Shallow that no man could better command his servants* (Henry IV part II 5.1)

custom NOUN custom is a habit or a usual practice ❏ *Hath not old custom made this life more sweet/ Than that of painted pomp?* (As You Like It 2.1)

cutpurse NOUN a cutpurse is an old word for a thief. Men used to carry their money in small bags (purse) that hung from their belts; thieves would cut the purse from the belt and steal their money ❏ *A cutpurse of the empire and the rule* (Hamlet 3.4)

dainty ADJ dainty used to mean splendid, fine ❑ *Why, that's my dainty Ariel!* (*Tempest 5.1*)

dally VERB if you dally with something you play with it or tease it ❑ *They that dally nicely with words may quickly make them wanton* (*Twelfth Night 3.1*)

damask COLOUR damask is a light-red or pink colour ❑ *Twas just the difference/Betwixt the constant red and mingled damask* (*As You Like It 3.5*)

dare 1 VERB dare means to challeng or, confront ❑ *He goes before me, and still dares me on* (*A Midsummer Night's Dream 3.3*) 2 VERB dare in this context means to present, deliver or inflict ❑ *all that fortune, death, and danger dare* (*Hamlet 4.4*)

darkly ADV darkly was used in this context to mean secretly or cunningly ❑ *I will go darkly to work with her* (*Measure for Measure 5.1*)

daw NOUN a daw was a slang term for idiot or fool (after the bird jackdaw which was famous for its stupidity) ❑ *Yea, just so much as you may take upon a knife's point and choke a daw withal* (*Much Ado About Nothing 3.1*)

debile ADJ debile meant weak or feeble ❑ *And debile minister great power* (*All's Well That Ends Well 2.3*)

deboshed ADJ deboshed was another way of saying corrupted or debauched ❑ *Men so disordered, deboshed and bold* (*King Lear 1.4*)

decoct VERB to decoct was to heat up, warm something ❑ *Can sodden water,/A drench for sur-reained jades*

... Decoct their cold blood to such valiant heat? (*Henry V 3.5*)

deep-revolving ADJ deep-revolving here uses the idea that you turn something over in your mind when you are thinking hard about it and so means deep-thinking, meditating ❑ *The deep-revolving Buckingham/ No more shall be the neighbour to my counsels* (*Richard III 4.2*)

defect NOUN defect here means shortcoming or something that is not right ❑ *Being unprepared/Our will became the servant to defect* (*Macbeth 2.1*)

degree 1 NOUN degree here means rank, standing or station ❑ *Should a like language use to all degrees,/ And mannerly distinguishment leave out/Betwixt the prince and beggar* (*The Winter's Tale 2.1*) 2 NOUN in this context, degree means extent or measure ❑ *her offence/Must be of such unnatural degree* (*King Lear 1.1*)

deify VERB if you deify something or someone you worship it or them as a God ❑ *all.. deifying the name of Rosalind* (*As You Like It 3.2*)

delated ADJ delated here means detailed ❑ *the scope/Of these delated articles* (*Hamlet 1.2*)

delicate ADJ if something was described as delicate it meant it was of fine quality or valuable ❑ *thou wast a spirit too delicate* (*The Tempest 1.2*)

demise VERB in this context demise means to transmit, give or convey ❑ *what state ... Canst thou demise to any child of mine?* (*Richard III 4.4*)

deplore VERB to deplore means to express with grief or sorrow ❑ *Never more/ Will I my master's tears to you deplore* (*Twelfth Night 3.1*)

depose VERB if you depose someone you make them take an oath, or swear something to be true ❑ *Depose him in the justice of his cause* (*Richard II 1.3*)

depositary NOUN a depositary is a trustee ❑ *Made you … my depositary* (*King Lear 2.4*)

derive 1 VERB to derive means to comes from or to descend (it usually applies to people) ❑ *No part of it is mine,/ This shame derives itself from unknown loins.* (*Much Ado About Nothing 4.1*) 2 VERB if you derive something from someone you inherit it ❑ *Treason is not inherited …Or, if we derive it from our friends/ What's that to me?* (*As You Like It 1.3*)

descry VERB to see or catch sight of ❑ *The news is true, my lord. He is descried* (*Anthony and Cleopatra 3.7*)

desert 1 NOUN desert means worth or merit ❑ *That dost in vile misproson shackle up/ My love and her desert* (*All's Well That Ends Well 2.3*) 2 ADJ desert is used here to mean lonely or isolated ❑ *if that love or gold/ Can in this desert place buy entertainment* (*As You LIke It 2.4*)

design 1 VERB to design means to indicate or point out ❑ *we shall see/ Justice design the victor's chivalry* (*Richard II 1.1*) 2 NOUN a design is a plan, an intention or an undertaking ❑ *hinder not the honour of his design* (*All's Well That Ends Well 3.6*)

designment NOUN a designment was a plan or undertaking ❑ *The desperate tempest hath so bang'd the Turks,/ That their designment halts* (*Othello 2.1*)

despite VERB despite here means to spite or attempt to thwart a plan ❑ *Only to despite them I will endeavour anything* (*Much Ado About Nothing 2.2*)

device NOUN a device is a plan, plot or trick ❑ *Excellent, I smell a device* (*Twelfth Night 2.3*)

disable VERB to disable here means to devalue or make little of ❑ *he disabled my judgement* (*As You Like It 5.4*)

discandy VERB here discandy means to melt away or dissolve ❑ *The hearts … do discandy , melt their sweets* (*Anthony and Cleopatra 4.12*)

disciple VERB to disciple is to teach or train ❑ *He …was/ Discipled of the bravest* (*All's Well That Ends Well 1.2*)

discommend VERB if you discommend something you criticize it ❑ *my dialect which you discommend so much* (*King Lear 2.2*)

discourse NOUN discourse means conversation, talk or chat ❑ *which part of it I'll waste/ With such discourse as I not doubt shall make it/ Go quick away* (*The Tempest 5.1*)

discover VERB discover used to mean to reveal or show ❑ *the Prince discovered to Claudio that he loved my niece* (*Much Ado About Nothing 1.2*)

disliken VERB disguise, make unlike ❑ *disliken/ The truth of your own seeming* (*The Winter's Tale 4.4*)

dismantle VERB to dismantle is to remove or take away ❑ *Commit a thing so monstrous to dismantle/*

So many folds of favour (*King Lear* 1.1)

disponge VERB disponge means to pour out or rain down ❑ *The poisonous damp of night disponge upon me* (*Anthony and Cleopatra* 4.9)

distrain VERB to distrain something is to confiscate it ❑ *My father's goods are all distrained and sold* (*Richard II* 2.3)

divers ADJ divers is an old word for various ❑ *I will give out divers schedules of my beauty* (*Twelfth Night* 1.5)

doff VERB to doff is to get rid of or dispose ❑ *make our women fight/ To doff their dire distresses* (*Macbeth* 4.3)

dog VERB if you dog someone or something you follow them or it closely ❑ *I will rather leave to see Hector than not to dog him* (*Troilus and Cressida* 5.1)

dotage NOUN dotage here means infatuation ❑ *Her dotage now I do begin to pity* (*A Midsummer NIght's Dream* 4.1)

dotard NOUN a dotard was an old fool ❑ *I speak not like a dotard nor a fool* (*Much Ado About Nothing* 5.1)

dote VERB to dote is to love, cherish, care without seeing any fault ❑ *And won her soul; and she, sweet lady, dotes, / Devoutly dotes, dotes in idolatry* (*A Midsummer Night's Dream* 1.1)

doublet NOUN a doublet was a man's close-fitting jacket with short skirt ❑ *Lord Hamlet, with his doublet all unbraced* (*Hamlet* 2.1)

dowager NOUN a dowager is a widow ❑ *Like to a step-dame or a dowage* (*A Midsummer Night's Dream* 1.1)

dowdy NOUN a dowdy was an ugly woman ❑ *Dido was a dowdy* (*Romeo and Juliet* 2.4)

dower NOUN a dower (or dowery) is the riches or property given by the father of a bride to her husband-to-be ❑ *Thy truth then by they dower* (*King Lear* 1.1)

dram NOUN a dram is a tiny amount ❑ *Why, everything adheres together that no dram of a scruple* (*Twelfth Night* 3.4)

drift NOUN drift is a plan, scheme or intention ❑ *Shall Romeo by my letters know our drift* (*Romeo and Juliet* 4.1)

dropsied ADJ dropsied means pretentious ❑ *Where great additions swell's and virtues none/ It is a dropsied honour* (*All's Well That Ends Well* 2.3)

drudge NOUN a drudge was a slave, servant ❑ *If I be his cuckold, he's my drudge* (*All's Well That Ends Well* 1.3)

dwell VERB to dwell sometimes meant to exist, to be ❑ *I'd rather dwell in my necessity* (*Merchant of Venice* 1.3)

earnest ADJ an earnest was a pledge to pay or a payment in advance ❑ *for an earnest of a greater honour/ He bade me from him call thee Thane of Cawdor* (*Macbeth* 1.3)

ecstasy NOUN madness ❑ *This is the very ecstasy of love* (*Hamlet* 2.1)

edict NOUN law or declaration ❑ *It stands as an edict in destiny.* (*A Midsummer Night's Dream* 1.1)

egall ADJ egall is an old word meaning equal ❑ *companions/Whose souls do bear an egall yoke of love* (Merchant of Venice 2.4)

eisel NOUN eisel meant vinegar ❑ *Woo't drink up eisel?* (Hamlet 5.1)

eke, eke out VERB eke meant to add to, to increase. Eke out nowadays means to make something last as long as possible – particularly in the sense of making money last a long time ❑ *Still be kind/And eke out our performance with your mind* (Henry V Chorus)

elbow, out at PHRASE out at elbow is an old phrase meaning in poor condition – as when your jacket sleeves are worn at the elbow which shows that it is an old jacket ❑ *He cannot, sir. He's out at elbow* (Measure for Measure 2.1)

element NOUN elements were thought to be the things from which all things were made. They were: air, earth, water and fire ❑ *Does not our lives consist of the four elements?* (Twelfth Night 2.3)

elf VERB to elf was to tangle ❑ *I'll ... elf all my hairs in knots* (King Lear 2.3)

embassy NOUN an embassy was a message ❑ *We'll once more hear Orsino's embassy.* (Twelfth Night 1.5)

emphasis NOUN emphasis here means a forceful expression or strong statement ❑ *What is he whose grief/Bears such an emphasis* (Hamlet 5.1)

empiric NOUN an empiric was an untrained doctor sometimes called a quack ❑ *we must not ... prostitute our past-cure malady/To empirics* (All's Well That Ends Well 2.1)

emulate ADJ emulate here means envious ❑ *pricked on by a most emulate pride* (Hamlet 1.1)

enchant VERB to enchant meant to put a magic spell on ❑ *Damn'd as thou art, thou hast enchanted her,/For I'll refer me to all things of sense* (Othello 1.2)

enclog VERB to enclog was to hinder something or to provide an obstacle to it ❑ *Traitors enscarped to enclog the guitless keel* (Othello 1.2)

endure VERB to endure was to allow or to permit ❑ *and will endure/Our setting down before't.* (Macbeth 5.4)

enfranchise VERB if you enfranchised something you set it free ❑ *Do this or this;/Take in that kingdom and enfranchise that;/Perform't, or else we damn thee.'* (Anthony and Cleopatra 1.1)

engage VERB to engage here means to pledge or to promise ❑ *This to be true I do engage my life* (As You Like It 5.4)

engaol VERB to lock up or put in prison ❑ *Within my mouth you have engaoled my tongue* (Richard II 1.3)

engine NOUN an engine was a plot, device or a machine ❑ *their promises, enticements, oaths, tokens, and all these engines, of lust, are not the things they go under* (All's Well That Ends Well 3.5)

englut VERB if you were engulfed you were swallowed up or eaten whole ❑ *For certainly thou art so near the gulf,/Thou needs must be englutted.* (Henry V 4.3)

enjoined ADJ enjoined describes people joined together for the same reason ❑ *Of enjoined penitents/*

There's four or five (*All's Well That Ends Well 3.5*)

entertain 1 VERB to entertain here means to welcome or receive ❏ *Approach, rich Ceres, her to entertain.* (*The Tempest 4.1*) 2 VERB to entertain in this context means to cherish, hold in high regard or to respect ❏ *and I quake,/ Lest thou a feverous life shouldst entertain/ And six or seven winters more respect/ Than a perpetual honour.* (*Measure for Measure 3.1*) 3 VERB to entertain means here to give something consideration ❏ *But entertain it,/ And though you think me poor, I am the man/ Will give thee all the world.* (*Anthony and Cleopatra 2.7*) 4 VERB to entertain here means to treat or handle ❏ *your highness is not entertained with that ceremonious affection as you were wont* (*King Lear 1.4*)

envious ADJ envious meant spiteful or vindictive ❏ *he shall appear to the envious a scholar* (*Measure for Measure 3.2*)

ere PREP ere was a common word for before ❏ *ere this I should ha' fatted all the region kites* (*Hamlet 2.2*)

err VERB to err means to go astray, to make a mistake ❏ *And as he errs, doting on Hermia's eyes* (*A Midsummer Night's Dream 1.1*)

erst ADV erst was a common word for once or before ❏ *that erst brought sweetly forth/ The freckled cowslip* (*Henry V 5.2*)

eschew VERB if you eschew something you deliberately avoid doing it ❏ *What cannot be eschewed must be embraced* (*The Merry Wives of Windsor 5.5*)

escote VERB to escote meant to pay for, support ❏ *How are they escoted?* (*Hamlet 2.2*)

estimable ADJ estimable meant appreciative ❏ *I could not with such estimable wonder over-far believe that* (*Twelfth Night 2.1*)

extenuate VERB extenuate means to lessen ❏ *Which by no means we may extenuate* (*A Midsummer Night's Dream 1.1*)

fain ADV fain was a common word meaning gladly or willingly ❏ *I would fain prove so* (*Hamlet 2.2*)

fall NOUN in a voice or music fall meant going higher and lower ❏ *and so die/ That strain again! it had a dying fall* (*Twelfth Night 1.1*)

false ADJ false was a common word for treacherous ❏ *this is counter, you false Danish dogs!* (*Hamlet 4.5*)

fare VERB fare means to get on or manage ❏ *I fare well* (*The Taming of the Shrew Introduction 2*)

feign VERB to feign was to make up, pretend or fake ❏ *It is the more like to be feigned* (*Twelfth Night 1.5*)

fie EXCLAM fie was an exclamation of disgust ❏ *Fie, that you'll say so!* (*Twelfth Night 1.3*)

figure VERB to figure was to symbolize or look like ❏ *Wings and no eyes, figure unheedy haste* (*A Midsummer Night's Dream 1.1*)

filch VERB if you filch something you steal it ❏ *With cunning hast thou filch'd my daughter's heart* (*A Midsummer Night's Dream 1.1*)

flout VERB to flout something meant to scorn it ❏ *Why will you suffer her to flout me thus?* (*A Midsummer Night's Dream 3.2*)

fond ADJ fond was a common word meaning foolish ❑ *Shall we their fond pageant see?* (*A Midsummer Night's Dream 3.2*)

footing 1 NOUN footing meant landing on shore, arrival, disembarkation ❑ *Whose footing here anticipates our thoughts/A se'nnight's speed.* (*Othello 2.1*) 2 NOUN footing also means support ❑ *there your charity would have lacked footing* (*Winter's Tale 3.3*)

forsooth ADV in truth, certainly, truly ❑ *I had rather, forsooth, go before you like a man* (*The Merry Wives of Windsor 3.2*)

forswear VERB if you forswear you lie, swear falsely or break your word ❑ *he swore a thing to me on Monday night, which he forswore on Tuesday morning* (*Much Ado About Nothing 5.1*)

freshes NOUN a fresh is a fresh water stream ❑ *He shall drink nought brine, for I'll not show him/Where the quick freshes are.* (*Tempest 3.2*)

furlong NOUN a furlong is a measure of distance. It is the equivalent on one eight of a mile ❑ *Now would I give a thousand furlongs of sea for an acre of barren ground* (*Tempest 1.1*)

gaberdine NOUN a gaberdine is a cloak ❑ *My best way is to creep under his gaberdine* (*Tempest 2.2*)

gage NOUN a gage was a challenge to duel or fight ❑ *There is my gage, Aumerle, in gage to thine* (*Richard II 4.1*)

gait NOUN your gait is your way of walking or step ❑ *I know her by her gait* (*Tempest 4.1*)

gall VERB to gall is to annoy or irritate ❑ *Let it not gall your patience, good Iago,/ That I extend my manners* (*Othello 2.1*)

gambol NOUN frolic or play ❑ *Hop in his walks, and gambol in his eyes* (*A Midsummer Night's Dream 3.1*)

gaskins NOUN gaskins is an old word for trousers ❑ *or, if both break, your gaskins fall.* (*Twelfth Night 1.5*)

gentle ADJ gentle means noble or well-born ❑ *thrice-gentle Cassio!* (*Othello 3.4*)

glass NOUN a glass was another word for a mirror ❑ *no woman's face remember/Save from my glass, mine own* (*Tempest 3.1*)

gleek VERB to gleek means to make a joke or jibe ❑ *Nay, I can gleek upon occasion* (*A Midsummer Night's Dream 3.1*)

gust NOUN gust meant taste, desire or enjoyment. We still say that if you do something with gusto you do it with enjoyment or enthusiasm ❑ *the gust he hath in quarrelling* (*Twelfth Night 1.3*)

habit NOUN habit means clothes ❑ *You know me by my habit* (*Henry V 3.6*)

heaviness NOUN heaviness means sadness or grief ❑ *So sorrow's heaviness doth heavier grow/ For debt that bankrupt sleep doth sorrow owe* (*A Midsummer Night's Dream 3.2*)

heavy ADJ if you are heavy you are said to be sad or sorrowful ❑ *Away from light steals home my heavy son* (*Romeo and Juliet 1.1*)

hie VERB to hie meant to hurry ❑ *My husband hies him home* (*All Well That Ends Well 4.4*)

hollowly ADV if you did something hollowly you did it insincerely ❑ *If hollowly invert/ What best is boded me to mischief!* (*Tempest 3.1*)

holy-water, court PHRASE if you court holy water you make empty promises, or make statements which sound good but have no real meaning ❑ *court holy-water in a dry house is better than this rain-water out o'door* (*King Lear 3.2*)

howsoever ADV howsoever was often used instead of however ❑ *But howsoever strange and admirable* (*A Midsummer Night's Dream 5.1*)

humour NOUN your humour was your mood, frame of mind or temperament ❑ *it fits my humour well* (*As You Like It 3.2*)

ill ADJ ill means bad ❑ *I must thank him only,/ Let my remembrance suffer ill report* (*Antony and Cleopatra 2.2*)

indistinct ADJ inseparable or unable to see a difference ❑ *Even till we make the main and the aerial blue/ An indistinct regard.* (*Othello 2.1*)

indulgence NOUN indulgence meant approval ❑ *As you from crimes would pardoned be,/ Let your indulgence set me free* (*The Tempest Epilogue*)

infirmity NOUN infirmity was weakness or fraility ❑ *Be not disturbed with my infirmity* (*The Tempest 4.1*)

intelligence NOUN here intelligence means information ❑ *Pursue her; and for this intelligence/ If I have thanks* (*A Midsummer Night's Dream 1.1*)

inwards NOUN inwards meant someone's internal organs ❑ *the thought whereof/ Doth like a poisonous mineral gnaw my inwards* (*Othello 2.1*)

issue 1 NOUN the issue of a marriage are the children ❑ *To thine and Albany's issues,/ Be this perpetual* (*King Lear 1.1*) 2 NOUN in this context issue means outcome or result ❑ *I am to pray you, not to strain my speech,/ To grosser issues* (*Othello*)

kind NOUN kind here means situation or case ❑ *But in this kind, wanting your father's voice,/ The other must be held the worthier.* (*A Midsummer Night's Dream 1.1*)

knave NOUN a knave was a common word for scoundrel ❑ *How absolute the knave is!* (*Hamlet 5.1*)

league NOUN A distance. A league was the distance a person could walk in one hour ❑ *From Athens is her house remote seven leagues* (*A Midsummer Night's Dream 1.1*)

lief, had as ADJ I had as lief means I should like just as much ❑ *I had as lief the town crier spoke my lines* (*Hamlet 1.2*)

livery NOUN livery was a costume, outfit, uniform usually worn by a servant ❑ *You can endure the livery of a nun* (*A Midsummer Night's Dream 1.1*)

loam NOUN loam is soil containing decayed vegetable matter and therefore good for growing crops and plants ❑ *and let him have some plaster, or some loam, or some rough-cast about him, to signify wall* (*A Midsummer Night's Dream 3.1*)

lusty ADJ lusty meant strong ❑ *and oared/ Himself with his good arms in lusty stroke/ To th' shore* (*The Tempest 2.1*)

maidenhead NOUN maidenhead means chastity or virginity ❑ *What I am, and what I would, are as secret as maidenhead* (*Twelfth Night* 1.5)

mark VERB mark means to note or pay attention to ❑ *Where sighs and groans,/ Are made not marked* (*Macbeth* 4.3)

marvellous ADJ very or extremely ❑ *here's a marvellous convenient place for our rehearsal* (*A Midsummer Night's Dream* 3.1)

meet ADJ right or proper ❑ *tis most meet you should* (*Macbeth* 5.1)

merely ADV completely or entirely ❑ *Love is merely a madness* (*As You Like It* 3.2)

misgraffed ADJ misgraffed is an old word for mismatched or unequal ❑ *Or else misgraffed in respect of years* (*A Midsummer Night's Dream* 1.1)

misprision NOUN a misprision meant an error or mistake ❑ *Misprision in the highest degree!* (*Twelfth Night* 1.5)

mollification NOUN mollification is appeasement or a way of preventing someone getting angry ❑ *I am to hull here a little longer. Some mollification for your giant* (*Twelfth Night* 1.5)

mouth, cold in the PHRASE a well-known saying of the time which meant to be dead ❑ *What, must our mouths be cold?* (*The Tempest* 1.1)

murmur NOUN murmur was another word for rumour or hearsay ❑ *and then 'twas fresh in murmur* (*Twelfth Night* 1.2)

murrain NOUN murrain was another word for plague, pestilence ❑ *A murrain on your monster, and*

the devil take your fingers! (*The Tempest* 3.2)

neaf NOUN neaf meant fist ❑ *Give me your neaf, Monsieur Mustardseed* (*A Midsummer Night's Dream* 4.1)

nice 1 ADJ nice had a number of meanings here it means fussy or particular ❑ *An therefore, goaded with most sharp occasions,/ Which lay nice manners by, I put you to/ The use of your own virtues* (*All's Well That Ends Well* 5.1) 2 ADJ nice here means critical or delicate ❑ *We're good... To set so rich a man/ On the nice hazard of one doubtful hour?* (*Henry IV part 1*) 3 ADJ nice in this context means carefully accurate, fastidious ❑ *O relation/ Too nice and yet too true!* (*Macbeth* 4.3) 4 ADJ trivial, unimportant ❑ *Romeo .. Bid him bethink/ How nice the quarrel was* (*Romeo and Juliet* 3.1)

nonpareil NOUN if you are nonpareil you are without equal, peerless ❑ *though you were crown'd/ The nonpareil of beauty!* (*Twelfth Night* 1.5)

office NOUN office here means business or work ❑ *Speak your office* (*Twelfth Night* 1.5)

outsport VERB outsport meant to overdo ❑ *Let's teach ourselves that honorable stop,/ Not to outsport discretion.* (*Othello* 2.2)

owe VERB owe meant own, possess ❑ *Lend less than thou owest* (*King Lear* 1.4)

paragon 1 VERB to paragon was to surpass or excede ❑ *he hath achieved a maid/ That paragons description and wild fame* (*Othello* 2.1) 2 VERB to paragon could also mean to compare with ❑ *I will give thee* bloody teeth If thou with Caesar paragon again/My man of men (Anthony and Cleopatra 1.5)

pate NOUN pate is another word for head ❏ *Back, slave, or I will break thy pate across* (The Comedy of Errors 2.1)

paunch VERB to paunch someone is to stab (usually in the stomach). Paunch is still a common word for a stomach ❏ *Batter his skull, or paunch him with a stake* (The Tempest 3.2)

peevish ADJ if you are peevish you are irritable or easily angered ❏ *Run after that same peevish messenger* (Twelfth Night 1.5)

peradventure ADV perhaps or maybe ❏ *Peradventure this is not Fortune's work* (As You Like It 1.2)

perforce 1 ADV by force or violently ❏ *my rights and royalties,/Plucked from my arms perforce* (Richard II 2.3) 2 ADV necessarily ❏ *The hearts of men, they must perforce have melted* (Richard II 5.2)

personage NOUN personage meant your appearance ❏ *Of what personage and years is he?* (Twelfth Night 1.5)

pestilence NOUN pestilence was a common word for plague or disease ❏ *Methought she purg'd the air of pestilence!* (Twelfth Night 1.1)

physic NOUN physic was medicine or a treatment ❏ *tis a physic/That's bitter to sweet end* (Measure for Measure 4.6)

place NOUN place means a person's position or rank ❏ *Sons, kinsmen, thanes,/And you whose places are the nearest* (Macbeth 1.4)

post NOUN here a post means a messenger ❏ *there are twenty weak and wearied posts/Come from the north* (Henry IV part II 2.4)

pox NOUN pox was a word for any disease during which the victim had blisters on the skin. It was also a curse, a swear word ❏ *The pox of such antic, lisping, affecting phantasims* (Romeo and Juliet 2.4)

prate VERB to prate means to chatter ❏ *if thou prate of mountains* (Hamlet 5.1)

prattle VERB to prattle is to chatter or talk without purpose ❏ *I prattle out of fashion, and I dote In mine own comforts* (Othello 2.1)

precept NOUN a precept was an order or command ❏ *and my father's precepts I therein do forget.* (The Tempest 3.1)

present ADJ present here means immediate ❏ *We'll put the matter to the present push* (Hamlet 5.1)

prithee EXCLAM prithee is the equivalent of please or may I ask – a polite request ❏ *I prithee, and I'll pay thee bounteously* (Twelfth Night 1.2)

prodigal NOUN a prodigal is someone who wastes or squanders money ❏ *he's a very fool, and a prodigal* (Twelfth Night 1.3)

purpose NOUN purpose is used here to mean intention ❏ *understand my purposes aright* (King Lear 1.4)

quaff VERB quaff was a common word which meant to drink heavily or take a big drink ❏ *That quaffing and drinking will undo you* (Twelfth Night 1.3)

quaint 1 ADJ clever, ingenious ❑ *with a quaint device* (*The Tempest 3.3*) 2 ADJ cunning ❑ *I'll... tell quaint lies* (*Merchant of Venice 3.4*) 3 ADJ pretty, attractive ❑ *The clamorous owl, that nightly hoots and wonders/At our quaint spirit* (*A Midsummer Night's Dream 2.2*)

quoth VERB an old word which means say ❑ *'Tis dinner time.' quoth I* (*The Comedy of Errors 2.1*)

rack NOUN a rack described clouds or a cloud formation ❑ *And, like this insubstantial pageant faded,/ Leave not a rack behind* (*The Tempest 4.1*)

rail VERB to rant or swear at. It is still used occasionally today ❑ *Why do I rail on thee* (*Richard II 5.5*)

rate NOUN rate meant estimate, opinion ❑ *My son is lost, and, in my rate, she too* (*The Tempest 2.1*)

recreant NOUN recreant is an old word which means coward ❑ *Come, recreant, come, thou child* (*A Midsummer Night's Dream 3.2*)

remembrance NOUN remembrance is used here to mean memory or recollection ❑ *our remembrances of days foregone* (*All's Well That Ends Well 1.3*)

resolute ADJ firm or not going to change your mind ❑ *You are resolute, then?* (*Twelfth Night 1.5*)

revels NOUN revels means celebrations or a party ❑ *Our revels now are ended* (*The Tempest 4.1*)

rough-cast NOUN a mixture of lime and gravel (sometimes shells too) for use on an outer wall ❑ *and let him have some plaster, or some loam,* *or some rough-cast about him, to signify wall* (*A Midsummer Night's Dream 3.1*)

sack NOUN sack was another word for wine ❑ *My man-monster hath drowned his tongue in sack.* (*The Tempest 3.2*)

sad ADJ in this context sad means serious, grave ❑ *comes me the Prince and Claudio... in sad conference* (*Much Ado About Nothing 1.3*)

sampler NOUN a piece of embroidery, which often showed the family tree ❑ *Both on one sampler, sitting on one cushion* (*A Midsummer Night's Dream 3.2*)

saucy ADJ saucy means rude ❑ *I heard you were saucy at my gates* (*Twelfth Night 1.5*)

schooling NOUN schooling means advice ❑ *I have some private schooling for you both.* (*A Midsummer Night's Dream 1.1*)

seething ADJ seething in this case means boiling – we now use seething when we are very angry ❑ *Lovers and madmen have such seething brains* (*A Midsummer Night's Dream 5.1*)

semblative ADJ semblative means resembling or looking like ❑ *And all is semblative a woman's part.* (*Twelfth Night 1.4*)

several ADJ several here means separate or different ❑ *twenty several messengers* (*Anthony and Cleopatra 1.5*)

shrew NOUN An annoying person or someone who makes you cross ❑ *Bless you, fair shrew.* (*Twelfth Night 1.3*)

shroud VERB to shroud is to hide or shelter ❑ *I will here, shroud till the dregs of the storm be past* (The Tempest 2.2)

sickleman NOUN a sickleman was someone who used a sickle to harvest crops ❑ *You sunburnt sicklemen, of August weary* (The Tempest 4.1)

soft ADV soft here means wait a moment or stop ❑ *But, soft, what nymphs are these* (A Midsummer Night's Dream 4.1)

something ADV something here means somewhat or rather ❑ *Be something scanter of your maiden presence* (Hamlet 1.3)

sooth NOUN truly ❑ *Yes, sooth; and so do you* (A Midsummer Night's Dream 3.2)

spleen NOUN spleen means fury or anger ❑ *That, in a spleen, unfolds both heaven and earth* (A Midsummer Night's Dream 1.1)

sport NOUN sport means recreation or entertainment ❑ *I see our wars/ Will turn unto a peaceful comic sport* (Henry VI part I 2.2)

strain NOUN a strain is a tune or a musical phrase ❑ *and so die/ That strain again! it had a dying fall* (Twelfth Night 1.1)

suffer VERB in this context suffer means perish or die ❑ *but an islander that hath lately suffered by a thunderbolt.* (The Tempest 2.2)

suit NOUN a suit is a petition, request or proposal (marriage) ❑ *Because she will admit no kind of suit* (Twelfth Night 1.2)

sup VERB to sup is to have supper ❑ *Go know of Cassio where he supped tonight* (Othello 5.1)

surfeit NOUN a surfeit is an amount which is too large ❑ *If music be the food of love, play on;/ Give me excess of it, that, surfeiting,/ The appetite may sicken* (Twelfth Night 1.1)

swain NOUN a swain is a suitor or person who wants to marry ❑ *take this transformed scalp/ From off the head of this Athenian swain* (A Midsummer Night's Dream 4.1)

thereto ADV thereto meant also ❑ *If she be black, and thereto have a wit* (Othello 2.1)

throstle NOUN a throstle was a name for a song-bird ❑ *The throstle with his note so true* (A Midsummer Night's Dream 3.1)

tidings NOUN tidings meant news ❑ *that upon certain tidings now arrived, importing the mere perdition of the Turkish fleet* (Othello 2.2)

transgress VERB if you transgress you break a moral law or rule of behaviour ❑ *Virtue that transgresses is but patched with sin* (Twelfth Night 1.5)

troth, by my PHRASE this phrase means I swear or in truth or on my word ❑ *By my troth, Sir Toby, you must come in earlier o' nights* (Twelfth Night 1.3)

trumpery NOUN trumpery means things that look expensive but are worth nothing (often clothing) ❑ *The trumpery in my house, go bring it hither/ For stale catch these thieves* (The Tempest 4.1)

twink NOUN In the wink of an eye or no time at all ❑ *Ay, with a twink* (The Tempest 4.1)

undone ADJ if something or someone is undone they are ruined, destroyed, brought down ❏ *You have undone a man of fourscore three* (The Winter's Tale 4.4)

varlets NOUN varlets were villains or ruffians ❏ *Say again: where didst thou leave these varlets?* (The Tempest 4.1)

vaward NOUN the vaward is an old word for the vanguard, front part or earliest ❏ *And since we have the vaward of the day* (A Midsummer Night's Dream 4.1)

visage NOUN face ❏ *when Phoebe doth behold/ Her silver visage in the watery glass* (A Midsummer Night's Dream 1.1)

voice NOUN voice means vote ❏ *He has our voices* (Coriolanus 2.3)

waggish ADJ waggish means playful ❏ *As waggish boys in game themselves forswear* (A Midsummer Night's Dream 1.1)

wane VERB to wane is to vanish, go down or get slighter. It is most often used to describe a phase of the moon ❏ *but, O, methinks, how slow/ This old moon wanes* (A Midsummer Night's Dream 1.1)

want VERB to want means to lack or to be without ❏ *a beast that wants discourse of reason/ Would have mourned longer* (Hamlet 1.2)

warrant VERB to assure, promise, guarantee ❏ *I warrant your grace* (As You Like It 1.2)

welkin NOUN welkin is an old word for the sky or the heavens ❏ *The starry welkin cover thou anon/ With drooping fog as black as Acheron* (A Midsummer Night's Dream 3.2)

wench NOUN wench is an old word for a girl ❏ *Well demanded, wench* (The Tempest 1.2)

whence ADV from where ❏ *Whence came you, sir?* (Twelfth Night 1.5)

wherefore ADV why ❏ *Wherefore, sweetheart? what's your metaphor?* (Twelfth Night 1.3)

wide-chopped ADJ if you were wide-chopped you were big-mouthed ❏ *This wide-chopped rascal* (The Tempest 1.1)

wight NOUN wight is an old word for person or human being ❏ *She was a wight, if ever such wight were* (Othello 2.1)

wit NOUN wit means intelligence or wisdom ❏ *thou didst conclude hairy men plain dealers, without wit* (The Comedy of Errors 2.2)

wits NOUN wits mean mental sharpness ❏ *we that have good wits have much to answer for* (As You Like It 4.1)

wont ADJ to wont is to be in the habit of doing something regularly ❏ *When were you wont to use my sister thus?* (The Comedy of Errors 2.2)

wooer NOUN a wooer is a suitor, someone who is hoping to marry ❏ *and of a foolish knight that you brought in one night here to be her wooer* (Twelfth Night 1.3)

wot VERB wot is an old word which means know or learn ❏ *for well I wot/ Thou runnest before me* (A Midsummer Night's Dream 3.2)